The OVERBERG

Inland from the tip of Africa

PREVIOUS SPREAD: Canola fields between Greyton and Riviersonderend, with the impressive Sonderend Mountains in the background (see p145). ABOVE: The towering sand dunes at De Mond Nature Reserve (see p104). OPPOSITE: Bot River Lagoon, looking towards the Perdeberg at Kleinmond (see p37). OVERLEAF LEFT AND RIGHT: Rolling fields of wheat stretch as far as the eye can see in the Caledon area (see p114).

First published in 2005 by Struik Publishers
(a division of New Holland Publishing (South Africa) (Pty) Ltd)
New Holland Publishing is a member of Johnnic Communications Ltd

London • Cape Town • Sydney • Auckland

Cornelis Struik House, 80 McKenzie Street, Cape Town 8001

ISBN 1 86872 992 3

10 9 8 7 6 5 4 3 2 1

Publishing Manager: Dominique le Roux
Managing Editor: Lesley Hay-Whitton
Senior Designer: Sian Marshall
Senior Editor: Michelle Coburn
Proofreader: Erika Bornman
Indexer: Ethné Clarke

Reproduction by Hirt & Carter Cape (Pty) Ltd
Printed and bound by Ajanta Offset

Additional photographs supplied by:
p10 top left, Elim water mill: Elim Heritage Centre; p78 top right, great white shark: Chris & Monique Fallows; p102 top and bottom, sweet potatoes and seafood: IOA/Neil Corder; p116 bottom, Boontjieskraal: Doreza & Uwe Kersandt; p123 middle left, Attie Fourie on commando: Attie Fourie; p177 middle left, Alwyn Zoutendyk: Marda Norris; p177 top right, mussels: IOA/Neil Corder; p179 middle left, Malgas pont: Marthinus Fouché; p181 right, wakeboarding on the Breede: Tides River Lodge; p182 bottom right, Breede River fish: Tides River Lodge; p191 bottom right, seafood *potjie*: IOA/Neil Corder; p191 middle left, southern right whale: SA Tourism; p196 top, mist on the Breede: Estelle Stodel; p202 (sepia photos), Zoutendyk family holiday photos: Marda Norris; p202 (black-and-white photos), Hermanus historic photos: Hermanus Old Harbour Museum.
IOA = Images of Africa

Acknowledgements

I would like to acknowledge and thank the following people for their time, hospitality, and encouragement: Greg and Louis from Zuurbraak, Braham van Zyl from the Hermitage Valley, Trevor and Marda Norris from Infanta, and Mariana and Peter Esterhuizen from Stanford. Many thanks are due to Wilfred Chivell and the crew from Dyer Island Cruises for the many trips out to sea so that I could get the perfect whale shot. Thanks also to Bob, Roanne and the staff of the Waenhuiskrans Restaurant, Phillycous and Herman from Caledon, and Kodak for film sponsorship. A warm thank you to my family and supportive friends. Above all I want to thank my husband and two dogs for their companionship, and my Father in Heaven who has created the Overberg and all its beauty. Particular thanks to Dominique, Michelle, Sian and all at Struik for publishing this book. – *Melanie Cleary*

The people I met in the Overberg were enormously generous with their time and their stories. They hauled out old family photographs, showed me their scrapbooks and fed me when it looked as though I was flagging. They took me to their favourite view spots, shared farming secrets and were honest and funny about life in the Overberg. How can I possibly thank you all enough? Writing this book has been a fantastic undertaking – one of those lifetime experiences that I won't ever forget. Each time I headed away from the city and my car began climbing Sir Lowry's Pass, I knew I was in for a treat. Thank you for making it so. The Struik team also deserves a round of applause for their encouragement, advice and their unshakeable belief that I could write a book like this in such a short space of time!
– *Karena du Plessis*

Contents

Hottentots Holland NR
HOTTENTOTS HOLLAND MTS
To Cape Town
N2
Viljoen's Pass
Sir Lowry's Pass
Eikenhof
Grabouw
Elgin
Steenbras Dam
Villiersdorp
Theewaterskloof
SONDEREND MTS
Genadendal
Sonderend
Riviersonderend NR
Greyton
Van der Stel's Pass
Dwarskloof Pass
GROENLAND MTS
Houhoek Pass
Bot River
Palmiet
Boontjieskraal
Gordon's Bay
Kogel Bay
HOTTENTOTS HOLLAND MTS
Kogelberg NR
Caledon
Shaw's Mountain Pass
Arabella
Hemel-en-Aarde Valley
Bot
Bot River Vlei
Rooiels
Pringle Bay
Betty's Bay
Kleinmond
Hawston
Fernkloof NR
Maanskyn-kop NR
KLEINRIVIER MTS
Jeslaarsdal
Klein
Akkedisberg Pass
Hermanus
Kleinriviersvlei
Vermont
Onrus
Sandbaai
Stanford
Hangklip
Walker Bay NR
Salmonsdam NR
ATLANTIC OCEAN
Walker Bay
Grootbos
De Kelders
Gansbaai
Danger Point
Franskraal
Kleinbaai
Baardskeerdersbos
Uilenkraalsmond
Wolvengat/ Viljoenshof
Pearly Beach
Dyer Island & Geyser Rock
Buffeljagsbaai
Die Dam
Quoin Point
LEGEND
Tarred Roads
Untarred Roads
Semi-tarred Roads
National Road
Rivers
Nature Reserves
De Mond NR
Mountains
POTBERG MTS
Villages & towns
Private resorts, farms & places

Bonnievale
LANGEBERG MTS
Marloth NR
LANGEBERG MTS
Barrydale
Grootvaders-bosch NR
Tradouw Pass
Breede
Buffel-jagsdam
Buffeljagsrivier
Zuurbraak
Swellendam
Bontebok National Park
Sonderend
Stormsvlei
N2
Heidelberg
Riviersonderend
R Û E N S
Protem
Breede
Klipdale
Malgas
Sout/Oukamma
Ouplaas/Wydgeleë
POTBERG MTS
Port Beaufort
Witsand
Infanta
De Hoop NR
De Hoop Vlei
Bredasdorp
Cape Infanta
INDIAN OCEAN
Kassiesbaai
Arniston/Waenhuiskrans
Soetendalsvlei
De Mond NR
Agulhas National Park
Struisbaai
L'Agulhas
Cape Agulhas
Johannesburg
CAPE TOWN
Swellendam
George
Port Elizabeth
CAPE TOWN
Swellendam
Caledon
George
CAPE TOWN
Swellendam

RIGHT: The village of Elim originated as a Moravian mission station in 1825. The Elim Heritage Centre has many historic photographs depicting life in the old days. FAR RIGHT: The Overberg is a fertile region producing everything from wine and wheat to canola and merino wool. OPPOSITE LEFT: The peaceful Buffeljags Dam between Swellendam and Zuurbraak. OPPOSITE MIDDLE: Kogel Bay on the stretch of coastline between Gordon's Bay and Rooiels. OPPOSITE RIGHT: Vanilla clothing store, Bredasdorp. Property prices in the Overberg are on the rise as increasing numbers of city escapees head for these small towns to open restaurants, shops and galleries. OVERLEAF: The Bot River Lagoon near Kleinmond, looking towards the Kogelberg Reserve.

Getting to know the Overberg

How can you not fall in love with an area that has some of the most lyrical names you can hope to find? There's Beard Shaver's Bush, Lizard Mountain Pass, Vale of Grace, Goose Bay, Pearly Beach, The Cellars, Sweet Valley Lake, River Without End and Sweet Anise Mountain. And that's just for starters! Welcome to the Overberg – that mysterious place 'over the mountains' that for centuries has represented many different things to different people.

Its boundaries begin as you climb Sir Lowry's Pass, and the region is bordered by the Sonderend Mountains and the coast up to Cape Infanta. Confused? Imagine a big egg-shaped region that includes Barrydale as its most far-flung settlement, then down to Witsand, and everything in between (see map on pp 8–9).

In the past it was the unexplored interior – full of possible danger and enormous potential. The first people who settled in the Overberg in the seventeenth century were of pioneering stock. They were the men and women who liked the space and freedom the remote mountains and windswept beaches afforded them. They loved the smell of the fynbos in the early morning as the sun warmed the rocks, and the sticky feel of the sea on their faces. They wanted to farm, to fish, to make their mark or to leave behind the complications of the city.

Today, we are equally passionate about the Overberg and escape there whenever we weary of city life and our spirits begin to dim. Whether your favourite place is a beach cottage at Franskraal, or a mountain retreat near Barrydale, it's the spectacular scenery, the quiet and the enormously friendly people that keep calling you back. Better yet, there are still places where you won't get cellphone reception and have absolutely no chance of buying a take-away dinner.

Today, much as before, the Overberg is inhabited by 'characters' – people who don't follow the mould, who want a different way of life and who couldn't be bothered to 'do the right thing'. There's the retired mathematics professor who is now passionate about proteas, or the old man who rides his horse 'on commando' for five days to get to the beach, or the young businesswomen who got sick of town politics and threw it all in to open a restaurant. Or there is the botanical artist who thinks in a hundred different shades of red, or the dedicated women who watch over the endangered African black oystercatchers. They are interesting, warm-hearted and generous. All you need to do is stand still for long enough and they'll give you a glimpse into their world. This, then, is what we wanted to offer you: a glimpse into a world we – and you – love.

We are a little concerned, however, that the people who get pride of place in this book are the *omies* of the Overberg. We looked for the *tannies*, but each time we went visiting they were 'in town shopping', 'working at the *tuisnywerheid*' or simply too busy to *kuier*. We only managed to corner a few but this certainly doesn't mean the women don't feature. We heard more than one story of the woman behind the man, the person who lent backbone to the family or was the real tough nut. On more than one occasion we were cautioned, 'Ooooh, you don't want to mess with *Tannie* Rina. She's the one who wears the pants in that family'. We didn't doubt it for one moment.

Here's a story that seems to capture the spirit of the area. Late one afternoon I went calling to try and find Uncle Eric in Swellendam. I don't know Uncle Eric but was told to ask for directions at the local garage. Before

long I was knocking on the door of his flat in the old age home. Uncle Eric was out but before I knew it, I was being grilled by his next-door neighbour – the feisty Lena Lourens. Now Lena is everything I've come to expect from the Overberg: strong and warm-hearted, overwhelmingly friendly and more than a little bossy. Within five minutes I had a cup of tea in my hand, had been offered a slice of Swiss roll and was accounting for myself as best I could.

Lena knows everybody and has been in the district for decades. This is the story she told me.

During the Depression, people in the Overberg were dirt poor. 'You would be amazed,' she said, 'what some of these women have done to survive. You might meet a real lady who is softly spoken with beautiful manners and a lovely hairdo, but in her time she could have hauled grain sacks weighing over 100 kilograms on and off wagons just to keep body and soul together.

'When I grew up we knew a woman who planted fields of *soetpatats*. She worked such long hours that her skin was burnt dark brown and her hands looked like claws. But her family survived, and when she got older her children treated her like a queen. She always had lovely clothes and her nightgowns looked like something from heaven. It's easy for some children to push their parents aside, but this never happened to her. I think her children realised what she had done for them and they were grateful until the day she died.'

I left Lena late that afternoon while the sun was setting. It was a tussle. Each time I got up to leave, Lena started telling me something else fascinating: the history of her farm, how she met her husband, and the trials and tribulations faced by farmers. 'It's getting late, child,' she said. 'You should stay for the night.' I know that, if I had agreed, Lena would have made a few phone calls and I would have had a bed for the night. And a *bord kos* and more irresistible stories.

Reluctantly, I dragged myself away. The sky turned pink and then an astonishing orange as though practising for an inspirational poster. I couldn't shake the image of a slender woman, on her hands and knees with her hands in the soil, willing her potato crop to flourish and grow. Then I drove past farms with the names Tevrede (Satisfied), Bo-vrede (More than Peace), Diamant (Diamond) and Dankbaar (Thankful). Clearly, these are people who have found their pieces of paradise.

As the light faded, the rain swept across the valleys. On either side of the highway, men were making the most of the wet and were ploughing their fields ready for the season's planting of rye, wheat, oats and barley. White birds milled around on the red earth and a herd of cows lined up outside a shed waiting to be milked. Labourers gathered around an outdoor fire to keep warm and, in the distance, it was possible to make out a homestead with a red roof guarded by towering blue gum trees. That night, as I drove past the apple co-op in Elgin, trucks were lined up in the dark waiting to deliver their fragrant loads.

I felt as though I had driven through the agricultural heart of the Western Cape – and mine had come out beating all the faster for it. This is the stuff that country songs are made of. These are the images that define a land and its people. This is the Overberg. – *Karena du Plessis*

Note: Every attempt has been made to portray people's stories as accurately as possible. But storytelling is a slippery fish, and we therefore apologise for any mistakes that may have crept in along the way.

Abundant Earth

GRABOUW, ELGIN and VILLIERSDORP

Pioneer to Celebrate
Golden Jubilee

1956

APPLES

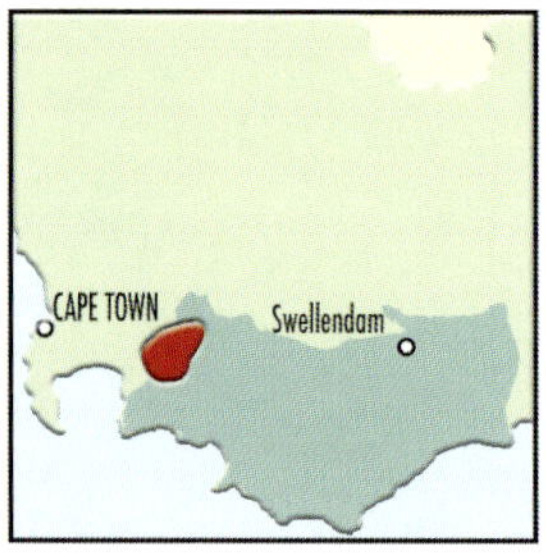

Welcome to Elgin and Grabouw and the beginning of the Overberg. Although this wonderful fruit-growing paradise is just a hop and a skip away from the city of Cape Town, once you're here, you'll feel as though you're in a completely different country and a world away from the hustle and hassle of urban life.

Spectacular
Grabouw & Elgin

The view from the top of Sir Lowry's Pass looking back over Somerset West and Cape Town is spectacular. There's the sweep of False Bay to the left and, in the distance, Devil's Peak towards the right. On a clear day, you can see all the way to Cape Point and the tip of the Cape Peninsula and, if the conditions are right, there will be a couple of foolhardy paragliders hovering above the road enjoying the thermals and revelling in the joy of being alive.

The ascent to the top of the Hottentots Holland Mountains wasn't always this easy. In 1655, when the first white men climbed the mountains in search of their fortunes, it was an exhausting scramble made all the more difficult by their trudge across the sandy *vlaktes* that now make up the sprawling area of the Cape Flats.

Of course these weren't the first explorers to trek over the mountains – the indigenous Khoekhoen people had been climbing up the range for centuries before, following the path travelled by the herds of eland and other wild animals that teemed on the plains below. The path was originally known as the 'Gantouw', the Khoekhoen word for eland, which acknowledges that the graceful antelope had picked out the best route long before cumbersome wagons had to be dismantled and hauled up and down the narrow track.

The first formal road was built in 1830 and named after the governor of the Cape, Sir Galbraith Lowry Cole, who devoted himself to building the pass as a way of linking the Cape with the interior. It was first tarred during the 1930s. Now the only hardship you are likely to face on this route through some of the prettiest countryside – known fondly amongst local residents as 'Groenland' ('Green Countryside') – is deciding whether or not to stop at all the tempting farmstalls, or just the one!

In spring the valleys of Elgin and Grabouw are postcard-perfect with rows upon rows of blossoming fruit trees, while during harvest time the air is redolent with the soft smell of apples. Huge trucks piled high with wooden crates packed with freshly-picked apples and pears trundle up and down the roads, and it would take a hard heart not to be moved by the overwhelming beauty of the misty blue hills ringing the estates that have been farmed by the same families for generations.

Just over 200 years ago, life across the Palmiet River (named for the palm-like reed *Prionium serratum* that grows along the river banks) was a lot less civilised than it is today. It took real adventurers to head out of town and start farming in the purple hills that have reminded more than a few of the Scottish moors. The first settlers were nothing more than subsistence farmers, and it was only at the beginning of the 1900s that far-sighted farmers began ploughing up their grain and vegetables in favour of the fruit trees for which Elgin and Grabouw are now world-famous.

Grabouw started off as a trading post in 1856 when an unknown artist from Cape Town, Wilhelm Frantz Ludwig Langschmidt, bought a farm and named it after Grabau, his birthplace in Germany. When Langschmidt settled there the small trading town instantly had a growing population because the artist had 23 children!

With Elgin there are two possibilities: one that the town was named after the Earl of Elgin (he of the Elgin Marbles notoriety). The alternative is that the area took on the name of a farm in the area, Glen Elgin, which was established in 1888 under a different name and then taken over in the early 1900s by the Molteno brothers.

You can't spend any time in the area without coming across names such as Molteno, Rawbone-Viljoen, Beukes and Cluver – founding families who have been in the area for centuries. The Molteno brothers, Ted and Harry, put Glen Elgin firmly on the map and there's a fantastic book, *Apples of the Sun* written by Phillida Brooke Simons, that chronicles the family history. By all accounts this was one of those exceptional tribes that spread all over the world, good at everything they turned their attention to and keen to make their mark in every aspect of life – from farming through to politics. But they were also a pretty strange bunch with more than their fair share of eccentricities and family dramas.

Small families were unheard of in those days and Edward (Ted) and Henry (Harry) were the seventeenth and nineteenth children of John Charles Molteno and Elizabeth Maria Jarvis. For all their differences in temperament, the two brothers made a very powerful team. Ted was more outspoken and domineering, but Harry was a natural farmer and Ted never made any decisions without consulting him first.

PREVIOUS SPREAD: The picturesque Theewaterskloof Dam near Villiersdorp (see p26) and other scenes from the region. LEFT: Apple picker, Elgin Valley. Harvest is a busy time of the year and provides people of the area with much-needed seasonal work. ABOVE: Wagon tracks left by the early pioneers can still be found carved into the rocks near Sir Lowry's Pass. RIGHT: Elgin and Grabouw are renowned internationally for the excellent quality of their fruit.

There's a wonderful story of the two men finishing their studies and deciding to go farming – inspired, no doubt, by their father's successful Karoo farms and their uncle's passion for fruit farming. To find the best property, Ted and Harry bought bicycles and cycled the length and breadth of the Cape, undeterred by bad roads, steep mountain passes and inclement weather. On their way back home from Swellendam at the turn of the 1900s, they visited Dr Antonie Gysbert Viljoen, a well-established farmer who was later elected to represent the Caledon district in the House of Assembly. Viljoen encouraged the Moltenos to buy a farm in the area that was up for sale, so they took the plunge, borrowed some money and bought Glen Elgin in 1903. Ted was 26 and Harry just 23 years old.

The brothers never married but instead channelled all their energy into farming, starting off – like everyone else in the valley – by growing potatoes and onions before switching to fruit. They were contrary fellows, hugely innovative in some areas and quaintly old-fashioned in others.

They wanted to farm as organically as possible and, instead of buying commercially-produced fertiliser, chose instead to ship in tons of kraal manure from the Karoo to fertilise their land. The men also spent an enormous amount of time and money trying to perfect the tricky business of cold storage to ensure that their fruit arrived in Britain in peak condition, and made tough decisions that kept them ahead of the game for decades. And, when the trees became worn out and stopped producing fruit, instead of ripping them out as other farmers in the area did, they simply left the old trees in peace and planted new tracts.

A family feud

The brothers never managed to shake off the irritation they felt for their young niece Kathleen Murray, who also started farming in the area. Hers is a remarkable story and her success says a lot about her determination and chutzpah. Kathleen certainly wasn't a conventional lass – but then pioneers seldom are. After studying in England at one of the first co-education boarding schools in the country, she returned to South Africa to visit her family. She was on the way back to England in 1914 to study agriculture at Cambridge when World War I broke out and she was forced to turn back.

Because Kathleen's options at the time were pretty limited, she didn't have much choice but to return to the family farm in Elgin and make a go of something the men in the family had failed dismally at – bee-keeping. At the beginning of 1915 Kathleen moved into Oak Lodge and, with the 35 pounds she had borrowed, bought her first beehives. She obviously had the magic touch as within a year her honey was winning awards at all the Cape agricultural shows and she quickly expanded into pig and poultry farming, which also won her accolades. Before 1915 was out, Kathleen had planted her first apple orchard. Initially the fruit trees were for the benefit of her bees, but, when it became clear that she was producing excellent fruit, she expanded her fruit-growing enterprise and also planted peaches and plums.

Kathleen's assistance came in the form of her Swiss friend, Mademoiselle Marguerite Genequand, an eleven-year-old child sent to her by the Child Life Protection Society, and one labourer – hardly an experienced team to get a farm off the ground, but that didn't seem to matter one bit. Kathleen also felt she had nothing to lose, so she took farming tips from whoever was offering them. She made friends with Dr Viljoen, attended several short courses at Elsenberg Agricultural College in Stellenbosch, and bought her trees from Harry Pickstone – the best nurseryman in the country and head of the sprawling Rhodes Fruit Farms where all the pioneering farmers bought their trees.

Although Harry and Ted Molteno had just started farming apples when Kathleen first arrived in the area, the brothers tried to warn her off farming in general and, more specifically, fruit farming.

Luckily, the young woman – she was in her early twenties when she started farming – decided to pursue her dream and went on to make a great success of it. One of her triumphs came in the mid-1920s when she was asked to supply apples for a huge South African exhibition taking place in England. Her fruit was chosen because it was obviously superior to most of the other fruit that was being produced at the time, and she sent it off with great aplomb, each apple carefully wrapped in tissue paper displaying her distinctive bee motif. And, later on, when Ted and Harry were tearing their hair out trying to ensure the fruit they exported to England got there in an edible state, Kathleen mastered this effortlessly.

Life often delivers up odd twists and turns and it was no different for these early apple farmers. Although both Ted and Harry remained bachelors all their lives, they did also have strong relationships with different women. One of the women Ted was close to was Kathleen Murray's friend, Marguerite Genequand, who lived with her at Oak Lodge. Although the reasons aren't clear, the two women fell out and Marguerite ended up living on Glen Elgin in a cottage Ted built for her. She is also buried alongside Ted on a Glen Elgin hillside overlooking the orchards.

Nothing can beat a Golden: crisp, juicy and exceptionally tasty.

RIGHT: As a young woman, Kathleen Murray defied convention and began farming in 1915. FAR RIGHT: Autumn leaves – each new season brings its own challenges for the farmers of the area. OPPOSITE: The Steenbras Dam, Grabouw, contains around 65 000 megalitres of water at full capacity and is an important source of drinking water for Cape Town.

In the beginning

The Moltenos weren't the only family to make their mark in the Elgin Valley. The Rawbone-Viljoens from Oak Valley are also intricately involved with life in the area and have farmed innovatively for decades. Although there's some debate about who should take the credit for planting the first fruit trees, records from Harry Pickstone's nursery suggest that it was Dr Viljoen, who placed the first order as early as 1899. By 1904 he already had 3 000 fruit trees and today 362 hectares are given over to apples and pears.

It's hard to imagine that Oak Valley Farm – which produces export-quality cut flowers, excellent wine, pasture-reared beef and top-quality fruit – was once considered a hopeless buy. In the biography of Dr Viljoen by Mignonne Breier, she describes how, in December 1898, an 'unprofitable stretch of land in an unfashionable area of the Caledon district' came under the hammer. Much to everyone's surprise, Antonie bought it for 4 000 pounds. The *Cape Times* reported that the doctor's friends 'severely rebuked him for his incalculable folly in buying a worthless bit of hungry sourveld in the despised Groenland'. What the sceptics didn't realise was that Dr Viljoen had a theory. He is reported to have said to his daughter: 'Nature never allows a vacuum.' He was confident something would grow in the area. It was just a matter of finding out what that was.

Of course farming in the early days wasn't without its difficulties. Viljoen's biography carries an excerpt taken from an article in the *Cape Times* in 1916, which describes just some of the hardships:

> *Sometimes when the winters are severe, the tigers (sic) in the French Hoek mountains descend to the sea and the sheep must* pas op. *One year one of the predatory gentlemen on his way via Houw Hoek down to the Palmiet mouth looked in upon the Senator's sheep. He leapt the fence, rounded up the adjacent flock, killed 24 by the throat and then resumed his journey. Next night over by Houw Hoek, he visited another farm and finished 17, making 41 sheep killed in two nights.*

But it wasn't all hard work. The Viljoens were a prominent family and there was a constant stream of visitors to their ever-expanding farm, ranging from Rudyard Kipling to General De la Rey – regarded as one of the South African War's great military leaders. They also regularly received the Molteno brothers, who used to arrive on their bicycles along with a strange sidecar contraption carrying their mother!

If ever farmers needed to make a plan it was during these early days, and stories about that period suggest that they were

wily and tough – and rarely deterred from getting what they wanted. During the South African War, Dr Viljoen was put under house arrest at Oak Valley for his support of the Afrikaners. As he wasn't allow to leave his farm, when he heard that a neighbouring farm, Glen Norman, was up for public auction, he managed to orchestrate that the event take place just behind his boundary line. Dr Viljoen bid from behind his hedge and, when he had secured ownership, flung open the gate that separated the two farms and walked onto 'his' property, confident that he wasn't breaking the terms of his house arrest.

Signs of the times

Farming in these beautiful valleys remains true to the past in many respects, but there are also plenty of changes afoot. As a nod to the past, sons still work alongside their fathers, learning from them, yet pushing for changes at the same time. Every year farmers hope for a cold, brisk winter that will stimulate an even blossoming in spring, and at the end of October everyone still watches out for the dreaded codling moth that can decimate an entire crop.

Whereas fruit farming in South Africa always used to be a lucrative business, significant changes in world markets and technology have shifted things. Sophisticated controlled atmosphere storage systems mean that good quality fruit is available all year round, and South African farmers have lost the advantage of being able to supply northern countries before anyone else.

Every year farmers wait anxiously to hear what prices they will be getting for their Royal Galas, Fujis and Pink Ladies. Apple varieties, like most things, go in and out of fashion. Granny Smiths, for example, are a bit passé these days. It appears as if global tastes are moving to sweeter apple varieties and the South African Golden Delicious remains a firm favourite in Europe due to its exceptional taste and sweetness. These are the trickiest of all apples to grow and the ones that bruise the quickest, making them difficult to handle and pack. But, if you get the growing of Goldens just right, says one farmer, who is as bent as an ancient apple tree, there is nothing to beat it: crisp, juicy and exceptionally tasty.

Perhaps the most significant change to the area, though, is the number of young farmers who are replacing orchards with vines. Suddenly every wine farmer is nosing around the area, excited about the cooler climate and the whisper of a sea breeze that comes off the coast. Traditional wine-growing areas like Stellenbosch and Franschhoek are getting hotter each year and more land is being gobbled up by housing estates.

'When I was growing up,' warned the bent apple tree farmer, 'nobody ever thought about wanting to live in Constantia.

OPPOSITE: Oak Valley Farm, known for its excellent fruit and cut flowers, has been in the Rawbone-Viljoen family for decades (see p20).
LEFT: The Elgin Valley isn't only known for its apples, but also for its top-quality pears. BELOW: To keep roses fresh, they should be picked early in the morning, and then plunged up to their necks in very cold water containing bicarbonate of soda.

The Houw Hoek Inn

There's some debate about how the Houw Hoek Inn got its name. One of the suggestions is that it's a corruption of the name Hout Hoek (Wood Corner), while others believe it comes from the cries of '*Hou!*' or 'Hold!' that wagon drivers would have shouted as they battled to negotiate the treacherous pass that was the undoing of many an early traveller. There's another idea suggesting that the word in fact derives from an old Khoekhoen word and means Kloof Corner.

The Houw Hoek Inn is one of the oldest licensed hotels in South Africa and must have been a welcome sight to exhausted travellers leaving and returning to the Mother City. Lady Anne Barnard stayed there in 1798 and wrote that the boiled chicken was fit for an emperor. Other early guests were pleased to find there were 'no louses' – always a good recommendation for any hotel.

More recently, the inn made a good outspan when the train stopped at the nearby station and passengers had to be served their meal on the station platform because of the brief stop. There's some mention of unscrupulous owners who made handsome profits by serving the soup course so hot that most diners were unable to eat it before the train had to leave again!

OPPOSITE: The Theewaterskloof Dam can hold 483-million cubic metres of water, but after a dry winter it's left worryingly empty. LEFT: The Houw Hoek Inn is one of South Africa's oldest hotels. TOP: Paul Cluver's vineyards play an important community role in the Thandi Empowerment Project (see p24). ABOVE: Henry May runs the Thandi Project's vegetable garden.

It was considered out-of-the-way and was sparsely populated by table grape growers. Now most of the farms and small-holdings have disappeared and it's just a fancy suburb. I've been living in the Elgin Valley for over 50 years and I've seen the changes. You're lucky if you break even these days but farming is a lifestyle that people find hard to give up, even if it isn't that profitable. Everyone is sub-dividing their farms and selling them off to people who want to escape from the city, and before long we're going to be just another suburb much like Constantia.'

Charles Hughes, CEO of Tru-Cape Fruit Marketing explains, 'When times are tough, as they have been in the recent past, growers question their planting mix and some opt to change. In the Grabouw Valley, as a result of climatic changes, sub-standard orchards are being replanted with wine grapes for which the climate is ideal. We are confident, however, that apples and pears will remain profitable, especially as the newer varietals produce fruit which is more in line with international taste trends.'

Coming up roses

Roses and flowers are as much a part of this area as the hectares of fruit trees. Each year hundreds of boxes of cut flowers and roses are sold to the rest of the country and exported overseas. If you're a rose fan and want to transform your garden, be sure to stop in at Duncan's Roses, which has been established on Arieskraal – one of the original farms in the area. Elgin Roses also sells gorgeous cut roses and you'll be tempted to buy them by the armful. For real inspiration, don't miss the area's annual open gardens, when gardeners display their talents. This takes place early each summer and you can pick up a map at any nursery in Cape Town or Somerset West and at local farmstalls.

The Paul Cluver Estate near Elgin has great shows in their amphitheatre during the summer. Also be sure to visit the Thandi Farmstore and buy some of their wines. The Thandi Project is a unique partnership between the state, the local community and private enterprise. Its aim is to empower the community by creating a sustainable business entity.

For something a little more energetic, explore the Hottentots Holland Nature Reserve, where the main attractions include fantastic mountain scenery, wild flowers and great pools for swimming. There are trails of varying lengths, including three day hikes as well as four overnight routes. A short trail has been laid out for the visually impaired.

Villiersdorp

Every old South African family has a story. So does every town. Villiersdorp – and the De Villiers who gave it their name – is no exception. The town is named after Pieter de Villiers, a local farmer who in 1843 set aside part of his farm, Radyn, to become the town. The De Villiers family became hugely influential in the development of the area and in shaping the history of the Cape.

When you visit Villiersdorp, stop at the Dagbreek Museum Restaurant where you can have something to eat and catch up on local history. There is a series of big black-and-white portraits in moulded frames and, in between *tee en koek*, you can't miss the portraits of Anna Elizabeth de Villiers and Petrus Norbertus Johannes Graaff that hang side by side. Therein lies a story that comes in a number of different shapes and forms, depending on who is doing the telling.

Legend has it that in the middle of the 1840s the young couple eloped on a white stallion and were finally caught in

The young couple eloped on a white stallion ...

RIGHT: Villiersdorp has always played an important role in the Overberg – both as an agricultural and historic centre (see text above). OPPOSITE TOP: A drive in the Overberg is never complete without stopping at one of the farmstalls for *padkos*, or to stock up on preserves, biltong and fine wines. The Thandi Farmstore on the Paul Cluver Estate is just one essential destination (see text above). OPPOSITE BOTTOM: The Houw Hoek Farmstall is not only popular for its delicious chicken and beef pies, but also hires out fishing rods and gear for anyone wanting to catch their own lunch in one of the dams or rivers in the area.

Moskonfyt (grape must jam)

When the grape market collapsed in the early 1920s, Villiersdorp farmers fell on hard times and needed to do something with their fruit. Moskonfyt, *an incredibly sweet grape syrup, was the result, and a* moskonfyt *factory was built in the area. It's easy to make.*

You need:
Sweet, ripe grapes – quantity adjustable depending on amount of liquid required
10 ml slaked lime per 5 litres grape juice

Remove the grapes from their stalks and crush them in a large bowl. Cover and leave to ferment for a couple of days. When the skins have risen to the surface, strain the juice through a sieve and add the slaked lime. Allow to stand for 30 minutes. Skim the juice and strain it. Heat the strained juice to boiling point in a large, heavy-based saucepan and strain it again. Return to the saucepan and boil rapidly, skimming the surface if necessary. Test the jam for setting point. It should have the consistency of thick syrup. Pour into hot, sterilised jars and seal. Be sure to leave some out to eat on fresh white bread with lashings of butter. (It should come as no surprise that, during her journeys through the Cape, Lady Anne Barnard is known to have commented that some of the burghers' wives were more than a little stout!)

Apple cake

This is one of the Rawbone-Viljoen family's favourite apple cakes that they've been making through the generations.

2 eggs
1 cup oil
1¾ cups sugar
2 cups flour
½ cup milk
½ t salt & 1 t bicarb
¼ t mace
½ t ground ginger
1 t baking powder
4 apples (unpeeled and cut into slices)
1 cup nuts
1 cup seedless raisins

Beat eggs well. Add oil and sugar and beat well. Add flour, milk and other dry ingredients. Fold in apple, nuts and raisins. Pour into well-buttered ring pan and bake at 180°C for 1 hour and 15 minutes. Sprinkle dry icing sugar over cake when cool.

There are moments of perfection wherever you look: a sheath of grass (ABOVE), a woman walking down a road with an armful of beautiful flowers (RIGHT) or a historic Villiersdorp fruit farm that has weathered many storms (OPPOSITE TOP). OPPOSITE BOTTOM: The Houw Hoek Inn, nestled beneath the Houw Hoek Mountain, is a popular conference venue (see p23).

Swellendam by Anna's outraged father, who brought them back home to his estate in the Villiersdorp area. De Villiers apparently wanted to charge Graaff with abduction – the old man's chief objection lay in the fact that Norbertus wasn't the gentleman he had imagined for his daughter, but rather was the family's groom. However, the magistrate managed to convince De Villiers that true love was more important and eventually persuaded him to allow the young lovers to marry.

The couple had a daughter, Hannie, who ended up working as a housekeeper in Cape Town for a family friend, the successful butcher, *Meneer* Combrink. Now, and this is where things get a bit woolly, it seems that Hannie had two much younger brothers, David and Jacobus, who were growing up *kaalvoet* and illiterate on the family farm before Combrink took an interest in the boys' schooling and brought them into town to study. As the boys grew up, they helped Combrink build up his business, which eventually became the well-known Imperial Cold Storage.

David was clearly a rising star and, at 22 years of age, became the Managing Director of this enormously successful company. In 1907 he donated land and 50 000 pounds for the establishment of the Sir David Graaff Institute – the local school in Swellendam. (He became a 'Sir' in 1910 when he was granted a baronetcy – a rank below that of a baron, but above that of a knight.)

Sir David proved his mettle as Cape Town's mayor and also served as a Cabinet Minister in both the Cape and Union Parliaments. He eventually married late in life and his son was the renowned Sir De Villiers Graaff, or Sir Div, as he was fondly known. He served as a Cabinet Minister in parliament, and finally as the leader of the opposition United Party in 1957. Sir Div was good friends with Jan Smuts and was eventually knighted for his philanthropy.

Exploring the area

The Theewaterskloof Dam is the seventh largest dam in South Africa and an important supplier of water to Cape Town. It's enormous – 52 square kilometres – and can hold 483 million cubic metres of water. The dam takes its name from the farm on which the dam wall is built and is great for bass fishing and other watersports. It is also possible to visit the Amandelhoutvlakte Bird Sanctuary by boat but visitors must obtain a permit from the Theewaters Sports Club.

In Villiersdorp itself you can get cultural by following the local art route and visiting artists in their home studios, or taking a self-guided walk around the town. The tourism bureau has a great map that gives wonderful insight into the fascinating history of Villiersdorp. You can also put your driving skills to the test and do one of the local 4x4 routes, the Stettyn Trail, which takes you through a beautiful historic wine farm.

If there's any time left, visit the Overberg Nursery and stock up on beautiful indigenous plants, or plan a hike in the Villiersdorp Wild Flower Garden and Nature Reserve, where the fynbos is exceptional and the birdlife abundant.

ABOVE: A small herd of horses explores the water's edge at the Theewaterskloof Dam, Villiersdorp (see p26). RIGHT: Local farm children find refuge in a leafy tree – the perfect hideaway on a hot summer's day. MIDDLE: The Houw Hoek Inn has been providing travellers with refreshment and comfort for decades. In days gone by, however, travelling through the Overberg was much more arduous than it is today. FAR RIGHT: Villiersdorp sunflowers provide a splash of yellow against the craggy backdrop of the Sonderend Mountains (see text box on p145).

Favourites

You can't leave the area without ...

- Taking a slow drive along some of the back roads during spring when the first blossoms are out and the orchards are awash with white and pink flowers.
- Buying a bag of freshly-picked apples from one of the farmstalls and relishing every bite.
- Catching the train! The Bot River Station Project is a fabulous way to explore the area. The train leaves from Cape Town station, stops at Somerset West and then goes through to Bot River. As it winds its way over the breathtaking Sir Lowry's and Houw Hoek passes, you will learn about the history of this railway line and be told more about the undiscovered pleasures of the Overberg.
- Cracking open an ice-cold can of Appletiser. This is Appletiser country, after all.
- Swooning over the magnificent roses at Fresh Woods during their open day in early summer.
- Stopping at Beaumont Wines at the foot of the Houw Hoek Pass. The farm Compagnes Drift used to be an outpost of the Dutch East India Company during the 1700s and, at one stage, stretched all the way down to the sea.
- Embarking on an adventure to find the tracks of the wagons that trundled up and down the punishing passes (see p16).
- Watching cricket (or, better still, playing a game) at the Elgin and Grabouw country club, which has to have one of the most magnificent settings in the country.
- Having lunch at the Dagbreek Museum Restaurant in Villiersdorp after taking in the collection of memorabilia and photos (see p24).
- Getting fit enough to do the Boland Hiking Trail and sleeping overnight in the hut. You'll revel in the peace and quiet.
- Hiring fishing rods and gear from the Houw Hoek Farmstall and trying your luck in one of the local dams or rivers.

Contact numbers

Elgin & Grabouw

Elgin & Grabouw Tourism: 021-859-1398
Air Team (Paragliding): 082-257-0808 or 082-727-6584
Beaumont Wines: 028-284-9733
Bot River Station Project: 028-284-9961 or 084-781-1983
Duncan's Roses: 021-848-9949
Elgin Apple Museum: 021-859-2042
Elgin & Grabouw Country Club: 021-859-3651
Fresh Woods: 021-844-0154
Hottentots Holland Nature Reserve (Boland Hiking Trail): 028-841-4826
Houw Hoek Farmstall and Coffee Shop: 028-284-9015
Orchard Farmstall: 021-859-2880
Paul Cluver Estate: 021-844-0605
Peregrine Farmstall: 021-848-9011
Thandi Farmstall: 021-844-0605

Villiersdorp

Villiersdorp Tourism: 028-840-0169
Dagbreek Museum Restaurant: 028-840-2126
Overberg Nursery: 028-840-1362
Stettyn Trail (4x4 route): 023-340-4453
Theewaters Sports Club (watersports): 028-840-1334
Villiersdorp Art Route: 028-840-0169
Villiersdorp Wild Flower Garden and Nature Reserve: 028-840-1130

Where to stay

www.overberginfo.com
Houw Hoek Inn: 028-244-9646
Huis de Villiers Guest House (Villiersdorp): 028-840-1386
Paul Cluver Guest House (Elgin/Grabouw): 021-844-0605
Rouxwil Farm (Elgin/Grabouw): 028-215-8922
Wildekrans Country House (Elgin/Grabouw): 028-284-9827

The pleasures of an orchard

'Oh how sweet and pleasant is the fruit of those trees which a man hath planted and ordered with his own hand, to gather it, and largely and freely to bestow and distribute it among his kindred and friends.'
– *Ralph Austen*

OPPOSITE TOP: Fires are essential for the regeneration of fynbos, as this is when the seeds of many species germinate. OPPOSITE BOTTOM: Like many other families, the Cluvers have been farming in this area for generations (see p16 and p24). ABOVE: Winding down after a long day in the fields on Oak Valley Farm. LEFT: Although it makes a spectacular photo, at the beginning of 2004 the level of the Theewaterskloof Dam was woefully low (see p26).

Where Sea and Stone Meet

KLEINMOND, BETTY'S BAY and PRINGLE BAY

RING BELL
TO ALERT
FOLLOWING
GOLFERS

Don't be fooled into thinking the stretch of coast from Rooiels to Kleinmond is the poor cousin to the more sophisticated Hermanus. Although less developed, this is one of South Africa's richest areas when it comes to flora – and its fans are determined to keep it that way. After all, you know you're in a special place when the supply store in Betty's Bay has a leopard-sighting poster pinned up next to the signs advertising discounted feta cheese.

Kogelberg Biosphere Reserve

The seaside villages of Rooiels, Pringle Bay, Betty's Bay and Kleinmond nestle adjacent to the Kogelberg Nature Reserve, which boasts some of the finest examples of mountain fynbos in the Western Cape and lies at the heart of the Cape Floral Kingdom. The Kogelberg's brag book reads like a naturalist's dream and, amongst other gems, includes 1 654 plant species (150 of which are considered endemic) and three patches of relic indigenous forest similar to the Knysna Forest. Local definitely is *lekker* and just some of the plants that were first identified in this area are *Erica patersonii*, *Nivenia stokoei*, *Erica pillansii* and *Erica banksii*. Given this incredible cornucopia, it's hardly any wonder that these small coastal villages are bristling with talented botanical artists who spend a lifetime trying to capture the beauty and diversity of the flowers around them.

It's a tough call but, when it comes to flora, pride of place has to go to the gorgeous red marsh rose or *vleiroos* (*Orothamnus zeyheri*) – a rare member of the *Proteaceae* family. It is the only species of its genus and is a perfect example of adaptability to what seem to be absolutely impossible conditions. It thrives in the howling gales that sweep across the Hottentots Holland Mountains and the seeds, which can lie dormant for many years, only come to life after fire. The marsh rose was nearly decimated by indiscriminate flower picking but, with strict controls now in place, it's beginning to make a comeback.

The area from Gordon's Bay to the east side of the Bot River Lagoon, and from the Groenlandberg to two sea miles off the coast, forms part of the Kogelberg Biosphere Reserve. This is a UNESCO initiative, which recognises that people – especially those communities living in close proximity to reserves or protected areas – can dwell in harmony with nature (see text box opposite). At the beginning of 2002, 94 countries had established 408 biosphere reserves, so being chosen to participate is a huge thumbs up for the Overbergers who live in the area – and a real acknowledgement of what they've done to keep it as unspoilt as possible. What's more, the Kogelberg is South Africa's first registered biosphere reserve and therefore serves as an excellent role model for other areas in the country that may be granted this status in the future.

How does the biosphere work? Best to think of an onion with its different layers. At the core of the Kogelberg is 18 000 hectares of wilderness. Conservation is a priority in this area and only low-impact activities such as hiking, cycling or bird watching are allowed. This core is buffered by more resilient and less ecologically sensitive areas and includes private and municipal reserves such as the Harold Porter National Botanical Garden, the Palmiet River, parts of the coast and the Bot River Lagoon. Beyond the reserve's borders, agricultural areas and towns make up a transitional zone. In this area the sustainable use of natural resources, including wild flower harvesting, fishing and alien tree plantations, is permitted.

PREVIOUS SPREAD: Kogel Bay and other scenes from the region. RIGHT: Kogel Bay, between Gordon's Bay and Rooiels, forms part of the Kogelberg Biosphere Reserve. FAR RIGHT AND OPPOSITE TOP: The Biosphere Reserve is home to 1 654 plant species. OPPOSITE BOTTOM: Hangklip, near Pringle Bay.

Outlaws and runaways

But things weren't always so rosy for this area of the Overberg. Not that long ago this rocky coastline with its towering mountains served as an inaccessible refuge for deserters, runaway slaves and outlaws who wanted to disappear from society. There was no scenic coastal road and the only pass over the Hottentots Holland Mountains was a gruelling track. So, even though Table Mountain and the Tavern of the Seas were visible in the blue distance, this hideaway was a world away and it was perfectly feasible for miscreants to disappear for years at a time.

It was a hard life and the bandits survived by hunting and stealing from local farmers. Although different versions of this story exist, in the late 1800s a group known as the Hangklip *Drosters* (Hangklip Deserters) attacked and killed a farmer and kidnapped his children. The illiterate outlaws wanted the children to write passes for them, so that they would be free to move around the Cape Colony again. But, rather than forging a pass, the young farmer's daughter wrote a rescue note instead. The *drosters* couldn't tell the difference and when the authorities came across the note they tracked down the kidnappers and launched a punishing attack. Forty-three men were killed and the children rescued.

This area presented many other perils, as many unfortunate sailors discovered. Cape Hangklip marks the eastern limit of False Bay, while the Cape of Good Hope marks the western limit. The two capes look so similar that Cape Hangklip became known by Portuguese navigators as Cabo Falso (The False Cape) because it was often mistaken for the more important, and safer, waters of the Cape of Good Hope. Lots of ships have run aground along this stretch of coast and there's even talk of the ghosts of children dressed in old-fashioned clothes running up and down the Rooiels beach on warm summer evenings.

Hangklip was also an important site for the British in World War II. Next time you have a cold beer at the Hangklip Hotel, raise a toast to the British servicewomen whose barracks it once was. They were responsible for operating a secret radar station from the mountain behind the hotel. This was just one of the stations around the world that were established by the Allies in their attempts to thwart Nazi expansion.

Getting the thumbs up

According to UNESCO guidelines, to qualify for designation as a biosphere reserve, an area should:

- be representative of a major bio-geographic region, including a gradation of human intervention in these systems;
- contain landscapes, ecosystems or animal and plant species that need to be conserved;
- provide an opportunity to explore and demonstrate approaches to sustainable development within the larger region where they are located;
- be of an appropriate size to serve the three functions of biosphere reserves: the core, buffer zone and outer-transitional area (see below and text opposite);
- have an appropriate zoning system with a legally constituted core area, or areas, devoted to long-term protection.
- have a clearly identified outer zone, or zones, and an outer transitional area.

Flowers and rugby players

Most people don't know that the unusual-looking, three-pronged flower emblem that adorns all the Western Province sports' team apparel – from rugby players through to horse riders – is, in fact, the *Disa uniflora*. This blood-red flower, which is part of the orchid family, is also known as the Pride of Table Mountain. There are currently 165 species of disa, which are only found naturally in Africa. Of these, around 135 species grow in southern Africa while the rest are found in the tropics.

Interestingly, at the beginning of 2004 a pretty pink-and-white new species was found in the Hex River Mountains. This has been sent overseas for verification and, who knows, soon there might be 166 species! These delicate orchids thrive in the coolness of cascades and waterfalls where they cling precariously to the faces of the rocks. Look out for the pretty mauve *Disa longicornu*, and the golden drops of *Disa cornuta* while you're hiking through Disa Kloof in the Harold Porter National Botanical Garden (see p44).

Kleinmond

Kleinmond took off in the 1860s when farmers from the interior started making the trek to the coast for their summer holidays. Much as they did in places like Infanta (see p187), they would arrive in their wagons, and later their trucks, and camp at the sea for a couple of weeks. A remnant of these holidays is the *Preekboom* (Preaching Tree) near the lagoon where families would gather for their church services and to celebrate Christmas Day. But in the mid-1800s there was also a small settlement of fishermen who had settled next to what is now the Kleinmond Harbour, where the fishing was good and there was plenty of fresh water. This community was known as Jongensklip but its members were forced to move from the area when the Group Areas Act was enforced during the 1960s. Today, the harbour has had a make-over that is part of the ongoing harbour development project, and includes restaurants, art galleries and shops.

The wild horses of the vlei

You don't just find wild horses in the Camargue or Mongolia – for as long as older Kleinmond residents can remember there have been feral horses living in the vlei between Rooisand Nature Reserve and the river mouth at Kleinmond. They're not strictly wild because they do come into contact with people, but they haven't been ridden or handled for at least 50 years – and this makes them pretty unusual.

Kleinmond resident Professor Frans van der Merwe is a retired animal nutritionist who is passionate about indigenous South African horses and has spent years doing genetic research on several breeds. He's also been keeping a close eye on the vlei horses for the last 30 years.

'The origin of these horses has given rise to a number of fanciful theories and romantic tales,' explains Van der Merwe. 'One of these is that they are the descendents of horses that were hidden from the British army during the South African War (1899–1902). In the age when we only keep horses for sport and recreation, people have forgotten how important these animals were to the development of South Africa. They helped shape our country's history and it is exciting to think the vlei horses might give us some clues about the horses of our past.'

But these animals aren't just significant from a historical point of view – they also play an important ecological role in the swampy estuary of the Bot River. They feed on a variety of edible plant species and also tread footpaths through the reed beds, which helps to keep the waterways open.

'You often see them grazing in the shallows, pushing their faces deep into the water to pull up tufts of water grass,' says Van der Merwe. 'They have adapted well to the wet and stormy Cape winters and grow thick, woolly coats to protect themselves against the cold. Most are light bay and many have a signature white star on their foreheads.'

In 2004, there were 16 individuals in the herd and, given that the horses don't move out of this area, they are all related. Despite the high degree of interbreeding, however, they are in remarkably good shape. Socially they behave the same as any true wild equids such as zebras or the wild desert horses of Namibia. Two of the six males in the present group are dominant and each maintains a separate harem. Two young bachelor stallions move between the sub-groups, taking care not to get too close to the dominant sires. When a mare comes into heat it is not uncommon for fierce fights to take place between the stallions and in the chaos young foals have been known to get hurt, or even killed.

The horses aren't fazed by people and there are wonderful photographs of these magnificent creatures nibbling on visitors' hats or simply standing close to them. This is one of Professor van der Merwe's concerns.

'They are tame, but they are also very unpredictable, so you never know when they could get a fright and flee from the area. It would also be a great shame if people started feeding these horses. They have adapted very well to their environment over the years, making this an exceptionally valuable herd genetically. You therefore don't want people to interfere with a delicate balance that clearly works.'

Vlei horses might give us a clue to the horses of our past …

OPPOSITE TOP: Disas are members of the orchid family and several species can be spotted in the Harold Porter National Botanical Garden at Betty's Bay (see p44). OPPOSITE BOTTOM: The feral horses living in the Bot River Lagoon have established an important role in the ecology of the estuary (see text above). RIGHT: Rooisand Nature Reserve at Kleinmond – home to a wealth of pristine fynbos and birdlife – forms part of the Kogelberg Biosphere Reserve. OVERLEAF LEFT: Tidal pool at Kleinmond. The surrounding area is popular for swimming, canoeing and fishing. OVERLEAF RIGHT: The vlei at Betty's Bay – a village where residents play an active role in conservation of the wildlife and fynbos.

Betty's Bay & Pringle Bay

Today, people flock to these small coastal villages to retire or relax for their holidays and there's still something of the *droster* spirit in many locals. After all, Betty's Bay and Pringle Bay were only electrified in the 1990s and early residents had to be hardy sorts who were happy to do their laundry by hand, or crank up a generator every time they wanted to watch television. These are also the Not in My Back Yard types who are quick to react to any threat to their way of life. The residents of Pringle Bay – named after Rear-Admiral Sir Thomas Pringle who commanded the British navy in Simonstown in the late 1790s – have put their muscle behind getting a proposal for a perlemoen hatchery turned down because of the impact it would have on the sensitive marine environment. And the Betty's Bayers have long resisted the instalment of streetlights because of the havoc they cause to the insect population. Of particular concern are the 'Mr Peabodies', bright green grasshoppery insects that don't stand a chance against bright lights and end up in papery piles punctuating the pavements of those villages that haven't managed to stave off as much development.

Jill Attwell, now in her eighties but 'without an ache in her body', is just one of the many residents with an indomitable spark. Her husband, Roelf, was one of the first people to buy a plot in Betty's Bay in 1938 and together they have seen the hamlet grow over the years. It was named after Betty Youlden, the daughter of the property developer who in the 1930s, together with Harold Porter and Jack Clarence, bought up farms in the area and formed a consortium that laid out the settlements of Rooiels, Pringle Bay and Betty's Bay.

Roelf first saw the pretty bay as a schoolboy when he hiked from Gordon's Bay to camp in the Rooiels Valley – not unusual, as the first holiday-makers used to send their provisions by boat while they hiked along the coast. This stretch wasn't always as accessible as it is today and, before World War II, there was just a rough footpath from Gordon's Bay to Rooiels. Jack Clarence was the main mover behind getting a proper road built and, during World War II, Italian prisoners of war were used to build Clarence Drive between Gordon's Bay and Kleinmond. With towering mountains on one side and the aquamarine ocean on the other, it must be one of the most breathtaking drives in South Africa.

The Attwells retired to Betty's Bay in the late 1970s. Or rather, retired from formal work only to take up a thousand other causes. They're particularly proud of being long-time members of The Hack, started by concerned residents in 1963 to tackle the *rooikrans* and hakea that was encroaching on 'their' fynbos. It takes place on the first Sunday of every month and, in over 40 years, has never been cancelled. The hack site is announced in the Kogelberg Botanical Society's monthly newsletter, or ask at the Harold Porter National Botanical Garden.

The Arabella Country Estate's five-star golf course is a golfer's paradise – the lagoon and mountains providing a breathtaking backdrop to the superbly manicured course landscaped with indigenous plants and fynbos. Afterwards you can relax in the fantastic spa or opt for a drink with a spectacular view. Be sure not to miss Arabella's monogrammed cappuccinos.

LEFT AND TOP: The Arabella Country Estate. ABOVE: Sacred ibises, as well as pelicans, fish eagles and various terns, are found in the Bot River Lagoon. OVERLEAF LEFT: An African black oystercatcher at Hangklip. OVERLEAF RIGHT TOP: Paper nautilus shells are found on the beaches of the Overstrand in winter. OVERLEAF RIGHT BOTTOM: Sunset at Kogel Bay, near Rooiels.

Nanny for a season

The African black oystercatcher is a familiar sight along this stretch of coast and, because holiday-makers always see a few birds on the beaches every year, they don't realise that there are only 5 000 of them left, and that they are endangered and have become an International Red Data species. These striking birds, with their all-black plumage and reddish-orange beaks and legs, breed from mid-November to the end of March and you'll find them as far north as Lüderitz in Namibia and Mazeppa Bay on the East Coast. Unfortunately their breeding season coincides with the busiest holidays, and the birds suffer as a result. They are an inter-tidal species and this confines them to the space between the rocky areas on the beach and the dunes.

Oystercatchers pair for life and they can live for up to 35 years. When the time comes for them to reproduce, the male makes a 'scrape', or nest – literally a dent in the sand above the high tide mark and far enough from the dunes to keep them safe from their predators. These include the mongoose, *rooikat* (lynx) and kelp gull, but humans, dogs and domestic cats are their most formidable enemies. The female lays two eggs, which take between 27 and 32 days to hatch. Both parents take it in turns to incubate the eggs. Sometimes the scrapes are artistically decorated with bits of shell, kelp or small stones and it's endearing to watch the male oystercatcher presenting his mate with a pretty bit of shell for decorating her home.

As soon as the chicks hatch they are hidden in the closest clump of kelp where they are perfectly camouflaged. They stay

Shell shock

Come winter, you'll have to get to the beach at first light if you want to find a treasured paper nautilus (*Argonauta argo*) shell. What's the rush? Well, the race is on between you and the wheeling, mewling gulls that don't have an eye for aesthetics, but rather smash the beautifully designed shells to get to the tasty bits inside.

For the technophiles, the nautilus is classified in the phylum *Mollusca*, class *Cephalopoda*, order *Octopoda*. Simply put, it's a member of the octopus family but, while the octopus has shed its outer shell and lives in rocky crevices, the paper nautilus has a unique shell that gives it all the buoyancy it needs for a life on the open seas.

The shell is actually a case for the eggs that the female secretes just before laying. Once her eggs are safely inside, she takes shelter in it and can usually be found with her head and tentacles peeping out. The male nautilus isn't as well-adapted as the female and not nearly as mobile because he isn't able to secrete his own shell. He is forced, instead, to hitch a ride with the female by squeezing into her mantle.

The mollusc's various names are as fanciful as it is, and they conjure up images of sailors, mythical voyages and distant lands. The name 'nautilus' comes from the Latin and Greek words for 'sailor' and was immortalised by Jules Verne as Captain Nemo's vessel in *20 000 Leagues Under the Sea*. The United States Navy used the same name for its first nuclear-powered submarine. The name 'Argo' comes from the ancient Greek legend of Jason who went in search of the Golden Fleece. His ship was named the *Argo*, and the brave men who volunteered to go with him on his heroic quest were known as the Argonauts.

there for a few hours while the parents lavish worms or tiny periwinkles and sand fleas upon them. An oystercatcher chick needs to be fully fledged and flying within 45 days of hatching, which adds up to a lot of hard work and attention from the parents. Within 24 hours of hatching the small chicks are taken onto the rocky outcrop that the parents have made their lifetime territory. However, oystercatchers who only have a vast expanse of beach with no rocks are at a disadvantage, as the chicks are more vulnerable to dogs and people. If humans come too close, the adult birds are prevented from feeding the youngsters and they become dehydrated.

Sara Starke, who lives in Betty's Bay, recognised the plight of the oystercatchers when she noticed that a pair, who had been trying unsuccessfully to bring a chick to maturity for the previous seven years on Main Beach, begin trying for the third time that breeding season to raise a family. Sara decided to give them a helping hand and she placed hazard tape and poles around the scrape. She also put up boards explaining the birds' predicament. To begin with Sara sat near the scrape during the very busy times on the beach. The birds got used to her being there and were soon christened Harold and Maude.

Most beachgoers didn't know much about oystercatchers and even fewer realised they were endangered. But, as time went by, the holiday-makers became accustomed to keeping their dogs under control and took a keen interest in the birds. And so the Oystercatcher Nannies of Betty's Bay was launched. Their main task is to guard the chicks when they are on the beaches at high tide and specifically during spring tides. The Nannies usually work in pairs to ensure maximum protection for the 10 breeding pairs in the Betty's Bay area. The success of the programme has inspired Pringle Bay residents to begin their own project to care for their two breeding pairs.

Once the oystercatcher chicks start to fly, they stay with their parents for a further two or three months, during which time the adults continue to feed them. This gives the young oystercatcher's beak time to fill out and become tough enough to prise open mussels and take limpets off the rocks. Watching an oystercatcher take a limpet out of its shell is a fascinating spectacle. The beak is used like a jackhammer to loosen the limpet, which is then cut in half and swallowed. Contrary to what the names suggests, the oystercatcher's diet consists mainly of limpets, mussels, red-bait, sand fleas, white mussels and worms.

Most chicks have to be forcefully evicted from the family group, but the parents don't chase them away until they have had exhaustive flying sessions. They're even given combat lessons because these youngsters will have to run the gauntlet of territories belonging to many other oystercatchers. When the chicks leave home they join 'clubs' of other young oystercatchers that they meet up with along the way. After about five to eight years the birds pair up and return to the place of their hatching to start a new episode of their lives.

The penguins of Stony Point

Stony Point – known for its towering dunes popular amongst sandboarders – has had various incarnations over the years. It's now known as a penguin breeding colony but for a while it was home to Cole's Southern Cross Whaling Company, which opened business in 1912. The company was liquidated just three years later but in 1917 Irvin and Johnson Ltd took over the whaling station and worked the seas until the Great Depression when the price of whale oil collapsed. In its heyday, however, about 300 whales were killed each year and the oil exported to Europe to be used for lighting and lubrication. The whaling station employed around 200 men – most of them Norwegians. It was finally closed in 1930.

It isn't clear why, but in the 1980s jackass penguins – known more formally as African penguins (*Spheniscus demersus*) – started breeding in the area. This is one of only two shore-based breeding colonies in southern Africa – the other more famous one is at the Boulders Beach near Simonstown.

Like oystercatchers, penguins mate for life and have been known to return to the same nesting site for up to 15 years. African penguins are regarded as an endangered species and there are thought to be around 170 000 birds left – just 10 percent of their population 60 years ago, which gives some indication of how rapidly the population has decreased. It has dwindled for a couple of reasons: the removal of bird eggs, declining fish stocks and disturbed nesting sites due to guano harvesting have all taken their toll. Attacks by domestic dogs and local leopards have also caused havoc but now this is a protected area. Boardwalks have been built at Stony Point so that visitors cause as little damage to the area as possible and you're not allowed to walk amongst the penguins.

Paradise in 'Shangri-la'

When Harold Porter bequeathed his 'Shangri-la' estate to the National Botanical Garden (today the South African National Biodiversity Institute) in 1958, he probably didn't realise just how valuable his gesture would be. The Harold Porter National Botanical Garden, in the heart of the Cape fynbos region, encompasses 10 hectares of cultivated fynbos garden and just over 190 hectares of pristine natural fynbos. So, depending on how energetic you're feeling, you can either do a gentle meander along carefully laid out paths, or some more rugged exploring and spot the magnificent *Disa uniflora* in its natural habitat (see text box on p36). There's even an area planted with salt-adapted plants – perfect inspiration if you're moving to an area that doesn't have great soil.

Of course, everyone wants to catch a glimpse of the legendary Betty's Bay leopard but these animals are so shy that you're unlikely to be so fortunate. However, this isn't the only trophy worth looking out for – of the bigger mammals there are also caracals and Cape clawless otters. Or you can lower your sights (but not your expectations) and seek out the shy little arum frog and Cape dwarf chameleon.

LEFT: A walk along the beach at Kogel Bay is the perfect antidote to the stress of city living.
BELOW: Pringle Bay, named after Rear Admiral Thomas Pringle, is famous for its rocky shores and the Drostersgat – a secluded cave used as shelter by runaways in the eighteenth century.
BOTTOM: Although Hangklip played an important role in World War II, any thoughts of conflict are long gone in this peaceful seaside resort.

Kreefbraai

There's nothing quite as satisfying as pulling out kreef *for your lunchtime braai, and Rooiels is one of the best spots to test your lungs and flex your diving muscles. The season is short-lived and runs for only a few weeks over Christmas and New Year – perfect timing for those blistering January days when all you want to do is hang around and drink cold beer. It's a short walk from your cottage down a dusty road and through the pungent fynbos before you hit the ocean with its slippery kelp and shocking coolness. Once you've got the* kreef *(only four per person each day at last count) preparation is a no-brainer.*

Kill the *kreef* by submerging in fresh water or plunging a diving knife through the shell and into the brain. Slice the tail down the back, clean under running water and place on medium coals. The trickiest part of the whole meal is making the perfect lemon-garlic butter and slapping it on while they cook. You'll know they're ready when the shell turns a bright orange and the flesh is white throughout rather than translucent. Be careful not to burn the shells, however, otherwise the meat will have a smoky, acrid taste. When they're done, flip the crayfish over for a flash on the flesh side to seal in the juices. Serve with wedges of lemon and salad. Only fingers allowed!

RIGHT TOP: Catching *kreef* for a lunch-time braai is an Overberg must. RIGHT: The tidal pool at Kogel Bay provides an early morning fisherman with a moment of quiet solace. OPPOSITE TOP LEFT: The king protea, or *Protea cynaroides*, is the largest member of the Protea family. It's South Africa's national flower and a close look at some of the country's money shows its majestic head embedded on the coins. OPPOSITE TOP RIGHT: Canoes can be hired at Kleinmond Lagoon for a lazy afternoon on the water. OPPOSITE BOTTOM: As it hugs the coast from Gordon's Bay to Kleinmond, Clarence Drive offers breathtaking views of False Bay.

Favourites

You can't leave the area without ...

- Going bird-watching in Rooiels (see p35). Amongst other species, be sure that you look out for the Cape rockjumper, orange-breasted sunbird, Cape sugarbird, Verreaux's eagle and Cape rockthrush.
- Taking a hike in the magnificent Kogelberg and keeping your eyes peeled for the elusive marsh rose (see p34).
- Having a swim in Jock's Bay and catching sight of a school of dolphins surfing the waves.
- Going on a guided walk with one of the volunteers at Harold Porter National Botanical Garden and learning to identify at least five different ericas (see p44).
- Taking a walk along the Kleinmond coastal paths while feeling the sea spray on your face (see p37).
- Volunteering to be an Oystercatcher Nanny (see p42).
- Horse-riding through the Bot River Lagoon in the hopes of catching sight of the feral horses (see p37).
- Sandboarding in the dunes at Stony Point. The views are breathtaking and it's an experience not to be missed.
- White water rafting on the Palmiet River in winter when the water is flowing strongly, or waiting for summer when the river is too low to go tubing.

ABOVE: Hangklip, with its variety of flora standing out against the granite rocks, is a nature lover's paradise. RIGHT: The mouth of the Palmiet River. It's possible to walk along the rocks from here to Kleinmond – great for whale watching along the way. OPPOSITE TOP: Fishing along this coastline is extremely popular. But when the waves are crashing it can also be very dangerous, as the crosses on the rocks attest. OPPOSITE LEFT: A dry vlei area at Kleinmond, Bot River Lagoon. OPPOSITE RIGHT: Kleinmond Harbour offers a selection of informal eating establishments, as well as art galleries and shops.

Contact numbers

Hangklip-Kleinmond Tourism: 028-271-5657
Arabella Country Estate (Bot River): 028-284-9383
Downhill Adventures (sandboarding): 021-422-0388
Gravity Adventure Group (paddling): 021-683-3698
Harold Porter National Botanical Garden: 028-272-9311
Kogelberg Nature Reserve (hiking): 021-945-4570
Kogelberg Biosphere Mountainbiking Trail: 028-271-5138
Rooisand Nature Reserve: 028-271-5657

Where to stay

www.overberginfo.com
Beach House B&B (Kleinmond): 028-271-3130
Bucaco Sud (Betty's Bay): 028-272-9750
Hangklip Hotel: 028-273-8448
Western Cape Hotel and Spa (Bot River): 028-284-0000

A piece of Heaven

HERMANUS, ONRUS and HEMEL-EN-AARDE VALLEY

DTC 1662
DEBBIE R27

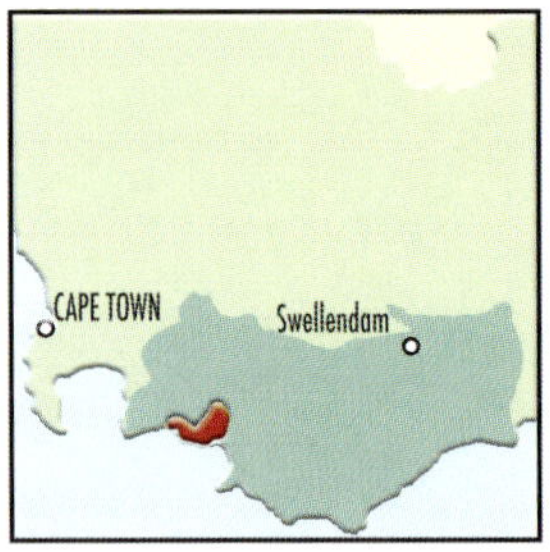

There's nothing to beat this coastline on a hot summer's morning, when you can smell the ozone and see the salt crystals suspended above the ocean. And, when you're standing on one of the cliffs with the sun on your face as you gaze over the blue sweep of ocean, it's very hard not to smile, for the area represents everything that is memorable about holidays: sunburnt shoulders, sandy feet and lazy afternoons.

Hermanus – the Riviera of the South

Now the rambunctious teenager of the Overberg – a bit glitzy and developing far too fast – Hermanus has some qualities that have endured. The mountains towering behind the town, the astonishing view that stretches for miles and the aquamarine sea have captured people's imaginations for centuries – and kept them coming back for more.

Hermanus wasn't always the chichi 'Riviera of the South'. Instead it was originally named Hermanuspietersfontein after Hermanus Pieters, a roving teacher and sheep farmer who came from the Netherlands and settled in Caledon around 1815. Hermanus married a local lass and the Pieters family moved to live on the farm Boontjieskraal – a landmark homestead in the Overberg, which you pass on the way to Caledon (see p114).

Each summer, after the arduous job of teaching the farm children to read and write, Hermanus Pieters would head for the coast with his sheep for a welcome break from the heat of the hinterland. There was a reliable spring, grazing was plentiful, fishing was good, and there were milkwood trees to shelter under. What more could a man want?

It wasn't long before others cottoned on to what Hermanus Pieters already knew, and in 1854 twelve plots were offered for sale by public auction in Caledon. They went for about one pound forty each and there was talk that the speculators had overpaid for infertile, rocky land that would be impossible to farm. At the time people weren't much interested in having a great sea view, and nobody was to know that these properties would form the hub of a burgeoning town that would transform itself from a rough-and-ready fishing village, into a fashionable resort town where properties fetch millions and the country's 'old money' come to relax. The town name was shortened to Hermanus at the beginning of the 1900s when the postmaster got tired of writing out the rather laborious Hermanuspietersfontein in his flowery script!

During her heyday in the first half of the 1900s, Hermanus was a firm favourite of the gentrified traveller, many of whom would arrive on the mailships that docked at Cape Town Harbour. The society column that was published in the local newspaper during the early 1950s captures the essence of the town and reads like an entry from *Debrett's Peerage & Baronetage* – the bible of who's who amongst British aristocracy. A shortened extract from Jose Burman's book, *Hermanus – A guide to the 'Riviera of the South'* reads:

PREVIOUS SPREAD: The Kleinriviersvlei at Hermanus, and other scenes from the area.
RIGHT: Hermanus's cliff path offers visitors the world's best land-based whale watching.
FAR RIGHT: Cape everlastings, also known as *sewejaartjies* (see p118), are exported for use in wreaths and dried flower arrangements.
OPPOSITE: The Old Harbour in Hermanus bears testimony to the hard lives many of the early fishermen experienced in the days before the town became a fashionable beach holiday resort.

TOP LEFT: The Hermanus market stocks everything from home-made preserves to artefacts from all over Africa. ABOVE AND TOP RIGHT: The Hermanus cliff path is the perfect place to escape for a quiet walk along one of South Africa's most beautiful coastlines. RIGHT: The Hermanus Lagoon, or Kleinriviersvlei. OPPOSITE: Grotto Beach has been named a Blue Flag beach (see p63) for its excellent facilities.

> *Sir Henry and Lady Horsman will be at the Riviera for a few months;*
> *General Sir Standish Crauford, and Colonel and Mrs Cavendish have arrived for their yearly stay;*
> *Lord Morley is expected this weekend;*
> *Sir Herbert Dunckerley is staying at the Bayview;*
> *Mrs Greta Hofmeyr had Lord and Lady Bicester to lunch;*
> *Lt. Col. Fitz-W. M. del Court is at the Marine;*
> *Sir Thomas and Lady Sopwith have arrived for their annual stay ...*

But, as fabulous as these times must have been with their dinner dances, big band music and the goings-on of the rich and famous, they weren't to last. The era of extended hotel vacations began to shift as more and more people bought their own holiday homes.

In the December of 1949 the local Hermanus newspaper carried an editorial by JO Rowe. In it he wrote:

> *I see with regret that no large-scale planning is advocated so far. I hope with all my heart that Hermanus will not become a city of casinos and gin-palaces, of great pavilions blocking out the glory of the sea coast; of wide concrete parades reflecting the heat of the sun and burning the eyes; of great motor roads tempting the young road-hog to devil-may-care antics with blasting horns and screeching brakes. There are other parts of the coast more suitable for attracting the noisy 'must-let-off-steam' bunch. Anyway Hermanus does not seem to be geographically suited for such attractions, for mercifully it is not on the way to anywhere special.*

The Marine

The Marine Hotel is one of those grand old ladies of the hotel industry that people return to year after year. When Walter McFarlane moved to Hermanus from Elgin in the 1880s, his initial business was fishing, but he found accommodation lacking and starting taking in guests at his cottage. Over the course of about 10 years his cottage expanded to become the Victoria Hotel.

McFarlane then built the Marine Hotel in 1902. It had just 21 rooms offering comfortable accommodation but no electricity or running water. The hotel did however have two flush toilets on each floor, which was considered the height of luxury!

The 1920s heralded the golden years of the hotel and its ballroom, where many rich and famous people danced in time to the beat of the big bands. However the fortune of the Marine waxed and waned for the next few decades until it was taken over in 1998 by hotelier Liz McGrath. She lovingly restored the hotel to its former glory and it is now part of the Relais & Chateaux group.

Legendary characters

Every town has its favourite sons and daughters, and Hermanus is no exception. The old Fisherman's Cottage just behind the Old Harbour has a nostalgic collection of black-and-white photographs chronicling the town's past. In amongst the memorabilia, it's impossible to miss the room devoted to Bill Selkirk who made a name for himself by catching sharks.

During the first half of the twentieth century, Hermanus became well known as an anglers' paradise and record catches were the norm. In 1950, for instance, a kabeljou caught at Klein Voëlklip was so heavy that it had to be towed ashore by four oxen. But these anglers weren't fishing for the pot as the Hermanus forefathers used to do. They were sport fishermen keen to pit their strength and endurance against big game fish.

In 1928 Selkirk made headlines when he landed a shark weighing over 1 000 kilograms – an unofficial world record. By the age of 50 he had reputedly caught 50 sharks, and had a lookout shed in the front of his house where he scanned the ocean for his next adversary. It's hard to imagine what he would make of the shark diving that's so popular today. If you want real adrenalin, he might argue, try wrestling with a monster of the deep, rather than just watching it swim on by.

Another character who helped make up the warp and weave of the town's fabric was Ella Gordon. She was an eccentric who lived up Karwyderskraal Road in the Hemel-en-Aarde Valley from the 1920s to the 1960s, long before it became a fashionable address. She built the school that served the local community, as well as her own cottage, which is still standing in a clump of gum trees down an unmarked road.

Gordon – originally from Scotland – prepared herself well for deepest, darkest Africa. She learnt to box and fight with a sword, wore her hair scraped back, smoked a pipe, and could easily lift a 200-pound sack of meal and lower it into her horse-drawn cart. Her greatest loves were her horses and donkeys. When one of them died she went into mourning and buried the animal in the horse graveyard near her cottage. The gravestones still stand and amongst the lichen you can make out her heartfelt farewells. One reads: 'Wickers: Trick Horse, Clever Good and True. Au revoir old friend from EGDC'.

Towards the end of her life Gordon was riddled with arthritis and her previously athletic body became as *krom* as a tree growing in the teeth of the southwesterly. After a stint in hospital in Cape Town, she demanded to be sent home. When she died, the story goes, she was so bent that the undertakers found it difficult to fit her into a coffin and resorted to putting a weight on her chest to counteract the damage the arthritis had caused. This seemed to work, but during the funeral service there was a resounding thud from the coffin, which cleared the church in the blink of an eye. The weight had rolled from its position, but the congregants suspected the irrepressible Miss Gordon would rise to live another 50 years up in the valley!

TOP LEFT: The Marine Hotel was established in 1902 (see p54). MIDDLE: The Hermanus cliff path follows the sea front between the New Harbour and the Kleinriviersvlei and offers incredible ocean and fynbos views. Some of the impressive homes that perch on the cliff, with outstanding views of the bay, are also a talking point. LEFT: The Hermanus Golf Club has an 18-hole par 73 parkland course (5 741 metres). ABOVE: View from the cliff path, which also has a section that's easily accessed by the physically disabled. RIGHT: The New Harbour, Hermanus. FAR RIGHT: Sieverspunt on the Hermanus cliff path.

Onrus

For decades, the tiny village of Onrus, at the base of the Onrustberge, has attracted a more bohemian crowd than its neighbours and has become something of an artists' colony. Just a few of the more famous painters and authors who have made their homes in the village are Jan Rabie, Marjorie Wallace, Gregoire Boonzaier, Elsa Joubert and Uys Krige.

It's hard to know exactly where the magic of Onrus lies. Is it the warm light on the mountain in the early evenings, the spray of white foam against a slick rock, or the smell of the fynbos on a hot afternoon? Perhaps it's a combination of all these wonderful things and more.

There's some confusion about the town's name. It isn't a bastardisation of Ons Rus (We Rest) as many people imagine. This would be perfectly fitting for a laid-back holiday town, but rather it is an abbreviation of 'Onrust', which means restless – and not really a feeling you want to be afflicted with while on holiday!

There are different explanations for the name – the wild and restless sea or dangerous river, the relentless wind, the disquiet residents originally felt at being so close to the leper colony in the Hemel-en-Aarde Valley, or the unease caused by the *drosters* who roamed the area (see p68 and p35 respectively).

For a time at the turn of the last century Onrus was a serious rival to Hermanus but, when one of the founding fathers invited Sir William Hoy (then in charge of the country's railways) to the area in an attempt to get him enthusiastic about building a railway from Cape Town to the coastal town, the move backfired on two accounts. Hoy came to Onrus, but stopped at Hermanus and fell in love with it instead. And he loved Hermanus so much that he refused to approve of a railway along the coast for fear that it would ruin the town's quaint character.

Present-day Onrus residents are probably thrilled that development passed them by in favour of Hermanus. There's something quirky about a town that has art galleries within walking distance of the beach and a tiny, tiny consecrated Greek chapel hidden amongst the milkwoods.

The lagoon is also a friendly spot – it's warmer than the sea, dogs and children can spend hours splashing in it without coming to any harm and there's a sweet restaurant right on the water's edge. Hello holidays!

Is it the warm light on the mountain in the early evening?

OPPOSITE TOP: Fly-fishing in the Hemel-en-Aarde Valley. OPPOSITE BOTTOM: Fick's Tidal Pool has its addicts who can't do without their early morning swim. ABOVE: A rickety jetty doesn't stop fishermen at Kleinriviersvlei, Hermanus, from setting out early each morning. RIGHT: The Marine Tidal Pool, below the Marine Hotel, is popular for swimming and snorkelling.

OPPOSITE: The Onrus Lagoon is ideal for children – warm, calm and safe. BELOW: The Orthodox Greek chapel in Onrus is nestled in a grove of milkwood trees. BOTTOM: Perlemoen, or abalone, is under threat in these waters due to poaching.
OVERLEAF LEFT: Mediterrea in Hermanus is the in place to be. Book a table near a window for a memorable meal. OVERLEAF MIDDLE: A characterful outbuilding behind the Hermanus tourist information office.
OVERLEAF RIGHT: Kleinriviersvlei, Hermanus.
OVERLEAF RIGHT PAGE: Grotto Beach is safe for swimming and is clean and well managed (see p63).

A scarce resource

You can't spend time along this coastline without having something to do with abalone. Whether it's diving for it, eating it, arguing about it or mourning its demise, this strange sea mollusc has shaped – and torn apart – the communities that hug the shores of the Overberg.

Abalone (*Haliotis midae*) is also known rather aptly as *klipkous* (rock sock). Its other name, perlemoen, is from the Dutch word '*paarlemoer*', or mother-of-pearl, which describes the shell's glorious inner lining. The mollusc thrives in areas of strong wave action and its flattened shape is perfectly designed to handle the push and pull of the ocean. Unfortunately, the fact that these shellfish develop in depths of around nine metres makes them sitting ducks for divers. And, because they only become sexually mature at between seven and eight years and reach full maturity at around 12 years, the resource doesn't stand a chance when undersized abalone are taken.

Chat to any Hermanus old-timer and they'll be able to tell you of a different time. The perlemoen divers of the 1950s and 1960s always had a certain mystery about them, but they were small-time players compared with the desperadoes and Cape Flats gangs currently involved in the black market trade. Back then, schoolboys made pocket money by packing the perlemoen in the bottom of the boats while the divers hauled them in. Today schoolchildren – and entire communities – are still being used extensively in the multi-million rand industry, but their involvement is not nearly as benign as it used to be. Now children under the age of 12, who are immune from prosecution, are being used as runners and they are often paid in the form of drugs.

But drugs aren't solely responsible for keeping the industry ticking over – there's big money involved as well. Prices vary enormously depending on demand and availability. A kilogram comprises about three perlemoen of legal size – and each of

Cooking with perlemoen

Everyone in this area has their own time-honoured way of preparing perlemoen. Or rather they have very fond memories of somebody else preparing it – and that seems to be the secret. Some people cut it into steaks and fry it in an egg batter, others chop it into pieces, stuff it into a tube of kelp and braai it, while still others mince it and make it into frikkadelle.

Before you get to the cooking phase, however, you've got to go through a lot of cleaning, scrubbing and banging with a meat tenderiser to make the poor mollusc taste like anything other than old car tyres. And, according to traditionalists, you aren't supposed to use salt or water during cleaning as this only toughens the muscular foot! One recommended way to prevent the possible Dunlop effect is to cook the abalone at a low heat overnight – making it more of a chore than a holiday delight. Another popular recipe suggests adding chicken soup, curry powder, a little Worcester sauce, some hot pepper sauce and then grating cheese on top of the whole lot – all of which suggests that overkill is the order of the day.

these is roughly as big as an adult's open hand. In the 1980s a kilogram of perlemoen sold overseas for between R30 and R80 but now the shellfish can sell for up to R1 400 per kilogram in the Far East. Estimates vary, but experts reckon that R400-million a year is being lost from South Africa.

Operation Neptune was launched in 1999 to help curb large-scale poaching. There have been successful prosecutions but this has proved to be a difficult task to manage because poaching is so embedded in many of the local communities. And, unfortunately, this marine police unit had to be shut down in 2004 due to a luck of funds.

'Poaching started escalating at a rapid rate in 1994,' explains Rob Tarr, Deputy Director of Inshore Resources at the Department of Environmental Affairs and Tourism. 'Estimates of the illegal catches are difficult to make, but range between 100 and 500 tons per year. The damaging effect comes, not only from the amount being taken, but importantly from the removal of undersized abalone that have not yet been able to reproduce. This practice can lead to species extinction. Sampling of confiscated material has shown that more than 50 percent of the abalone being taken are undersized.'

But poaching isn't the only culprit responsible for the declining figures. Tarr goes on to explain that Cape rock lobsters (*Jasus lalandii*) moved into the inshore coastal region between Hangklip and Hermanus in the early 1990s.

'This resulted in the lobsters consuming virtually the entire population of sea urchins,' explains Tarr. 'The urchins provide an essential hiding place for juvenile abalone and now that there are no urchins left, this has left the abalone exposed to predation. Juveniles have virtually disappeared between Hangklip and Hermanus, which means it is unlikely that this area will be able to support any future sustainable abalone fishery as long as the lobster abundance remains high.'

Fly the blue flag

Grotto Beach in Hermanus is one of the few beaches in South Africa to have previously been given Blue Flag status – a prestigious international award granted to selected beaches that fulfil certain strict criteria.

The Blue Flag is an exclusive eco-label given to beaches and marinas in countries across Europe and South Africa that meet high environmental standards, as well as offer good sanilary and safety facilities. The 14 requirements that have to be met include excellent water quality, environmental education and information, environmental management, together with high safety standards and services. If some of these specifications are not fulfilled during the season for which the award is granted, the Blue Flag award is withdrawn.

The international Blue Flag campaign includes environmental education for decision-makers and members of the public, as well as tourism operators.

Giants of the deep

In recent years Hermanus has no longer closed up shop for the winter months as it once used to do, because this is the whale season. From late May onwards, everyone scans Walker Bay for the first sighting of a shiny black fluke or V-shaped spray. Until October, thousands of visitors flock to the cliff path above the Old Harbour, which offers one of the best views in the world for land-based whale watching. This is a far cry from the days when the whaling stations at Betty's Bay and Donkergat were slick with the blood of these magnificent creatures (see p44).

The whale you're mostly like to spot is the southern right whale (*Eubalaena australis*). The whale's name says it all – this was the 'right' whale to hunt because it was rich in oil and baleen and floated when killed, making it easy for the whalers to retrieve the dead creatures. The southern rights were so ideal, in fact, that they would almost certainly have been hunted to extinction if it hadn't been for an international treaty that came into effect in 1935, providing them with protection.

The estimated current global population of southern right whales is between 2 000 to 4 000 individuals – up from about 100 in 1935. However this represents only about ten percent of the number of southern rights that used to frequent our waters before they were hunted. The population grows by about seven percent every year, meaning that it doubles every ten years. The number of southern right whales should be back to what it used to be in 2040.

The Hermanus whale crier

Next time you see a bit of old kelp washed up on the shore, spare a thought for Wilson Salukazana, the world's only whale crier and one of Hermanus' top tourist attractions. Then, see what sound you can manage to coax out of the twisted bit of seaweed!

Wilson took over the job as whale crier five years ago when Pieter Claasens, who was first appointed to the job at the beginning of the 1990s, resigned due to ill health. Because Wilson grew up in Hermanus, the whales weren't strange to him and he had been keeping a close eye on them for years.

Wilson worked first at the Birkenhead Hotel, 'back in the days when there were many fine hotels in Hermanus,' and then trained as a community guide.

'I learnt many useful things in my course, but *I* had to teach *myself* how to blow my kelp horn,' laughs Wilson. 'I have learnt how to make the horns and shape them in different ways. Because the horns are hollow, you don't get a huge variety in sounds out of them – you need to cut small holes in the kelp if you want to change its tone.

'I don't have a favourite whale,' continues Wilson. 'During winter and spring when they start to mate there can be as many as 700 or 800 whales in the bay at one time, but the average is between 60 and 70 per day. It is very exciting when you see the first blow of the season and their huge tails lifting out of the water confirming their presence. I've come to recognise some, with their white patches and grey colours, but there are usually too many to single them out.'

Keep your ears open for the mournful blast of the whale crier's kelp horn. Different calls made up of long and short 'blows' will let you know where whales have been spotted:

New Harbour	– •
Preekstoel	• •
Fick's Pool	– –
Old Harbour	– • –
Roman Rock	• • •
Kwaaiwater	– – –
Voëlklip	• – •

See what sound you can coax out of the twisted bit of seaweed.

The secrets of whale language

- BREACHING involves leaping out of the water with an arching back-flip.
- GRUNTING sounds almost like a roar and can usually be heard kilometres away.
- LOBTAILING means slapping the tail flukes on the surface of the water.
- SPYHOPPING involves standing vertically with head and body, as far as the flipper, above the surface, allowing the whale to get a clear view of its surroundings.

Every Overberger needs some handy whale facts for impressing visitors ...

- Southern right whales can measure up to 18 metres and may weigh more than 54 000 kilograms.
- They spend the summer months down south, feeding in the icy waters of the Antarctic, before heading up north to warmer waters to mate, calve and raise their young.
- The whales return every year between the end of May and early July to give birth to a single calf after a gestation period of about a year.
- To sound like an old sea salt you need to be able to tell your humpback from your southern right. You can recognise the southern right by its characteristic V-shaped blow. Humpbacks have a dorsal fin and are usually smaller than the southern rights. They are black or grey in colour, with a lighter underbelly.

OPPOSITE: Wilson Salukazana, the world's only whale crier.
TOP RIGHT, ABOVE AND RIGHT: A southern right whale lobtailing and breaching (see text box above).
OVERLEAF: Changing moods of the lagoon at Hermanus, known as the Kleinriviersvlei or Stofvlei.

Hemel-en-Aarde Valley

The Hemel-en-Aarde (Heaven and Earth) Valley wasn't always a sought-after address. From 1817 to 1846 it was a leper colony and a place of great suffering. Nobody is entirely sure how it got its name, but it could have been the sense of desolation early settlers experienced in the valley – when they looked up, all they could see were the mountains and sky.

When the first case of leprosy was diagnosed in Stellenbosch in 1756 there was enormous misunderstanding surrounding the disease, and the afflicted were shunted from one remote corner of the country to another in order to keep them away from healthy people. Lord Charles Somerset was responsible for establishing the leper colony in the Hermanus area and lepers were sent to a farm called Hemel-en-Aarde in Attaquas Kloof. The farm belonged to a widow, Susan Niemand, who also had leprosy, and a settlement of huts and vegetable gardens was established. At the end of 1820 there were more than 100 patients living in the colony – not always very happily either, as a number of the lepers ran away.

The conditions at the leper colony were far from ideal: food was scarce, living conditions prison-like and medical treatment virtually non-existent. Salvation came in the form of Dr James Barry, a British army doctor, who was appalled by the suffering he found. He persuaded Somerset to improve the patients' diets and also recommended that those strong enough should swim in the sea every day. This was in direct contrast to the previous ruling that had banned sufferers from going down to the coast in case they contaminated healthy residents.

But, although life at Hemel-en-Aarde improved enormously after Dr Barry intervened, in 1823 the government insisted that healthy children and spouses of sufferers be separated from the lepers and so, in that year, 27 children were taken from their parents and sent to the mission station at Genadendal (see p147). The healthy adults were the next to go and eventually the whole leper colony was disbanded and the remaining sufferers sent to Robben Island in 1846.

The curious life of Dr Barry

Dr James Barry served in the British army in far-flung corners of the world for over 40 years as an extremely competent doctor. However, there were always questions surrounding his gender and the uncertainty continues today, 140 years after his death in Malta. Some reports claim Barry was a woman who had so badly wanted to be a doctor, that she had managed to pretend that she was a man for most of her life. But other experts say that all the evidence points to Barry being a hermaphrodite. Barry's life was the subject of much gossip and was marked by sexual scandals, a fiery temper, extravagant dress and far-thinking ideals. He was admired for his quick thinking, an ability to keep a cool head in difficult situations, and is famed for having introduced the Caesarean section to Africa. His blistering temper, however, was easily provoked, especially when anyone made fun of his high-pitched voice!

Heavenly wines

The Hemel-en-Aarde Valley of today is nothing like the sad place it used to be. Now it's Walker Bay's wine ward with some of the country's best wines coming from farms such as Bouchard Finlayson and Hamilton Russell. This is the premiere area for growing the capricious Pinot Noir grape – the varietal that frustrates wine growers, wine makers and drinkers alike because it's so fickle.

Favourites

You can't leave the area without ...

- Having a leisurely lunch at The Milkwood at Onrus after a morning on the beach or next to the lagoon (see p59).
- Finding a seascape you simply can't live without in one of Onrus's galleries.
- Swimming in the tidal pool below the landmark Marine Hotel. You'll be hard-pressed to find such a fantastic view anywhere else (see p54).
- Losing count of the whales from the cliff path while eating ice-cream – even though the winter winds are howling and your nose is frozen.
- Listening to the haunting call of the famous Hermanus whale crier (see p64).
- Finding a perlemoen shell in a rock pool and tucking it into your suitcase to take back home with you.
- Fishing off Kraal Rock and braaiing your catch for dinner that evening.
- Visiting top quality wine farms in the Hemel-en-Aarde Valley (see p68).
- Exploring Fernkloof Nature Reserve. There are over 40 kilometres of paths to discover so you'll never get bored.
- Falling asleep in your swimming costume after a punishing morning spent reading a magazine on your porch overlooking the ocean.
- Taking in the stunning view from the Rotary Way. Drive along this scenic route above Hermanus for breathtaking views across the sea to Danger Point. Adventure seekers can also do a tandem paragliding flight.
- Visiting the Old Harbour Museum for insight into the history of the village.
- Visiting a perlemoen hatchery for an educational tour and learn more about this strange and precious mollusc.
- Taking a guided walking tour through the nearby township of Zwelihle, where you can have a traditional Xhosa meal, visit an African healer and meet some of the local residents.

PREVIOUS SPREAD TOP LEFT: Vineyards in the Hemel-en-Aarde Valley thrive in the cool sea climate. TOP MIDDLE AND RIGHT: Hamilton Russell wine estate is known for its Pinot Noir and delicious Chardonnay. BOTTOM LEFT: View of the Steenboksberg, Hermanus. BOTTOM CENTRE: Dam in the Hemel-en-Aarde Valley. BOTTOM RIGHT AND CENTRE: Fernkloof Nature Reserve – a fynbos paradise and home to 1 500 plant species. THIS SPREAD FAR LEFT TOP TO BOTTOM: Scenes from the Maanschynkop Reserve . TOP MIDDLE AND RIGHT: Views from the Hermanus cliff path. LEFT: The Hermanus Yacht Club at Kleinriviersvlei is the ideal location for messing about in boats. The lagoon is tidal but when the Cape winds blow, you can fly on the water!

ABOVE: Kwaaiwater, on the Hermanus cliff path, means 'angry waters' – and it's not hard to see why. RIGHT: The New Harbour, Hermanus. FAR RIGHT: Fick's Tidal Pool, Hermanus. OPPOSITE TOP LEFT: The Auberge Burgundy is just one of the excellent guest houses in the seaside town that offer visitors world-class service and accommodation. OPPOSITE BOTTOM LEFT: Hermanus's New Harbour is a working harbour that's home to the local branch of the National Sea Rescue Institute. OPPOSITE FAR RIGHT: The famous Hermanus cliff path hugs the coast for kilometres and changes its mood with the seasons.

Contact numbers

Hermanus

Hermanus Tourism: 028-312-2629
De Wet's Huis Photo Museum: 028-313-0418
Fernkloof Nature Reserve: 028-313-8100
Fishermen's Cottage: 028-312-3642
Hermanus Abalone Hatchery: 028-312-2140
Hermanus whale crier, Wilson Salukazana: 028-312-2629 or 073-214-6949
Hermanus Whale Cruises: 082-369-8931
Mogg's Country Cookhouse: 028-312-4321
Old Harbour Museum: 028-312-1475
Rotary Way (paragliding): 082-257-0808 or 082-727-6584
Southern Right Charters (whale watching): 082-353-0550
Zwelihle Township Tour: Call Wilson Salukazana (see above for telephone number)

Hemel-en-Aarde

Bouchard-Finlayson: 028-312-3515
Hamilton Russell: 028-312-3595 or 312-1791
Sumaridge Wines: 028-312-1097

Onrus

The Milkwood: 028-316-1516

Where to stay

www.overberginfo.com
Auberge Burgundy: 028-313-1201
Birkenhead Hotel: 028-314-8000
Marine Hotel: 028-313-1000
The Artist's House: 028-313-0533
The Windsor Hotel: 028-312-3727

Salty Seadogs & Quiet Hamlets

GANSBAAI, STANFORD, FRANSKRAAL, and BUFFELJAGSBAAI

BOKKIE
ELECTRICAL
HARDWARE
LIGHT FITTINGS
FLOOD & SPOT LIGHTS
GAS
HEATERS & STOVES
OUTDOOR REQUIREMENTS
KEYS CUT HERE
Hout R7
NO PARKING

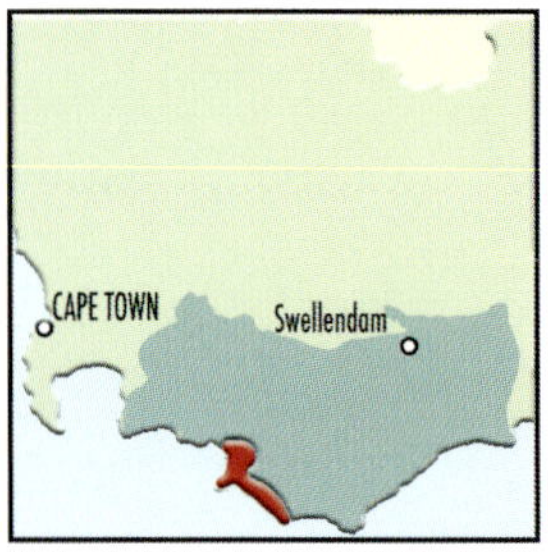

The stretch of coast from Stanford to L'Agulhas is an intoxicating alchemy of the elements. There's the smell of the sea, the feeling of salt on your skin and the sound of the waves in their endless ebb and flow. Then there are the mountains, the coastal fynbos, the noisy seabirds and — always — the fish. This is seaside bliss.

Down-to-earth

Gansbaai

The graveyard at Gansbaai has one of the best views in the country. It's a stone's throw away from jagged rocks and the blue, blue ocean that shifts and heaves with slick fronds of kelp. The early graves are simple mounds decorated with perlemoen shells. By way of contrast, there's a weathered wooden cross from around 1920 and a smart new marble ship's wheel and anchor on Dan Bokkie's grave. There can be little doubt that these are people who lived and died by the sea – the salty brininess as much a part of them as the blood that coursed through their veins.

Gansbaai, like De Kelders, Franskraal and Pearly Beach, is an odd mixture of retirees, permanent residents and holiday-makers. There are rusty Land Rovers parked in the driveways and always lots of men standing around in shorts, rubbing their beer *boepe* while taking stock of the sea and sky. The children ride their bikes up and down the quiet streets and there's plenty of messing about in boats at the harbour.

Not all that long ago, however, Gansbaai (Goose Bay) looked quite different from this. The fishermen lived in rudimentary thatched cottages just above the high-water mark with their rowing boats pulled up out of reach of the licking waves. Most of the cottage roofs were secured with poles or stones to protect them from the wind and the ridges were protected by perlemoen shells set close together. Unfortunately, these cottages were destroyed in the 1960s to make way for the new harbour, but there are photos in the local fish shop that speak of a different time when every man knew the ebb and flow of the tides like he knew the back of his hand. Later on, the boats were named after the geese that made this bay famous and on a rough day, when it was too dangerous to head out to sea, you could find the *Rietgans*, *Stormgans*, *Sneeugans*, and *Riviergans* moored in the harbour.

Although people had been visiting here since the late 1700s, the formal settlement began in around 1880 on the farm Strandfontein. There's some debate about whether or not the early residents of Gansbaai were survivors of the *Birkenhead* (see p80), but that seems unlikely as most of them were found after a couple of days and any surviving shipwrecked soldiers were soon packed off to war.

Today, people come from around the world to go shark diving off Gansbaai and Kleinbaai. Between Dyer and Geyser Island is the famous Shark Alley – a name that speaks for itself. The islands are home to Cape fur seals and jackass penguins – a perfect food supply for great white sharks.

Steamed mussels

Spending a lazy holiday at the coast is the perfect excuse to pull on your scruffy old takkies *and head to the beach for some mussel picking. Once you've got your quota, head home, pour a cold glass of wine or beer and leave the mussels to soak in clean cold water for just over an hour. After they've soaked, throw out those that float or open and scrape off any stringy, beardy bits and scrub them well. There are a million ways to cook mussels: grilled on the braai, as a soup, or steamed with white wine and cream sauce.*

The recipe is really easy:

Chop an onion, some celery, garlic and a carrot really finely and sauté these slowly in butter. Don't do this over a high heat as you want the onions soft and translucent rather than crisp. When those ingredients are soft, turn up the heat, throw in the mussels and add a good amount of white wine. How much you add will depend on the number of mussels you want to cook. Put the lid on and let the mussels steam for five minutes. Now pour in some cream and finely chopped flat-leaf parsley and let this boil up with the lid off. The mussels are best eaten in a soup bowl so you can have lots of sauce over them. You'll need plenty of crusty bread to mop up the juices. (Don't eat the mussels that haven't opened!)

Diving with sharks

There's nothing like a close encounter with a great white shark to get your heart racing. It is a combination of things that will soon have you giggling like a schoolgirl and babbling like a baby: the boat ride to the dive spot, the anticipation of adventure, the first cold rush of water as you lower yourself into the briny deep and then the silent glide-by of a magnificent animal that will remind you that you're alive. Although there are lots of tall stories, the biggest great whites are usually around six metres long. Shark populations are declining at alarming rates and over-fishing for delicacies such as shark fin soup are to blame. Great whites are protected in South African waters, meaning it is illegal to catch or kill them, or to trade with their jaws and other body parts.

OPENING SPREAD: Village street in Stanford and other scenes from the region. PREVIOUS SPREAD LEFT: Fisherman, Gansbaai. PREVIOUS SPREAD RIGHT: De Kelders near Gansbaai is named for the famous Klipgat and Druip Kelders caves in the cliffs. THIS SPREAD TOP LEFT AND ABOVE: Gansbaai Harbour is a busy fishing port and has a modern canning factory for processing fish. RIGHT TOP AND BOTTOM: Dyer Island is home to thousands of Cape fur seals that provide great white sharks with a constant food supply. OPPOSITE TOP AND BOTTOM: Changing moods at Uilkraalsmond Reserve. OVERLEAF TOP LEFT: Mariana Esterhuizen serves her famous Overberg chicken pies at her restaurant in Stanford. OVERLEAF BOTTOM, TOP MIDDLE AND FAR RIGHT: Scenes from Mariana's in Du Toit Street, Stanford.

Caving in

De Kelders (The Cellars) near Gansbaai is best known for the caves after which the village was named. The Duiwelsgat hiking trail is well worth doing and will take you through Klipgat and Druip Kelders – caves that are on every archaeologist's to-do list. Lady Anne Barnard visited the caves in 1798 but they were only excavated in the 1960s. While it's hard to make real sense of enormous time differences, it's fascinating to know that in Klipgat the archaeologist Frank Schweitzer of the South African Museum found artefacts, fauna and some human teeth left by Middle Stone Age people from between 40 000 to 80 000 years ago. Schweitzer also discovered shell middens of Later Stone Age Khoekhoen pastoralists who were living in the Western Cape between 1 600 to 2 000 years ago.

Stanford

This pretty little village that hugs the banks of the Klein River was named after Captain Robert Stanford. As early as 1798, the British Colonial Secretary at the Cape, Mr Andrew, and Lady Anne Barnard visited the farm Kleinriviersvallei on their first trip into the interior. Even then it was a good place to be – the grazing was plentiful, the river calm and constant and the mountains in the distance gave the settlement an extremely attractive outlook.

Stanford bought the farm in 1838 when he retired from the British Army on half pay and made a living by supplying the Cape with fresh meat, fruit and vegetables. Things came unstuck for him in 1849, however, when the British government made the highly controversial decision to establish a penal colony at the Cape.

Not surprisingly, emotions were running high when *HMS Neptune* docked in Cape Town with the first batch of convicts, and the settlers at the Cape refused to supply the ship with fresh food. Although Sir Robert agreed with their sentiments, because he was still employed by the Crown he believed it was his duty to give the British authorities what they needed. He therefore broke ranks and supplied the convict ships with the necessary provisions.

The consequences were dire. People stopped doing business with him, the banks refused to lend him money and his labourers were chased off his farm. Stanford's family members were pelted in the streets and, very tragically, his sick child was refused medical treatment and subsequently died.

The farm was eventually sold by public auction to Phillipus de Bruyn in 1855 and it didn't take him long to start subdividing it into plots for what was later to become the town.

There's some debate about whether the town was named after Stanford out of British gratitude for his self-sacrificing decision, or whether he paid De Bruyn 50 pounds sterling for the honour but, either way, Stanford lost the land he loved by doing what he believed was the honourable thing.

However honour was a big thing back then and that's exactly why the *Birkenhead* became so famous. In 1852, just before Stanford had to sell his farm to pay off his creditors, a British frigate carrying reinforcements for the Eighth Frontier War in the Eastern Cape collided with Danger Point near Gansbaai. Within minutes the ship began to sink but instead of rushing for the lifeboats, the soldiers and sailors were ordered to 'stand fast', and they lined the decks while the women and children were escorted to safety. There are reports of men keeping rank while waist-high in water and then shaking hands with their friends and colleagues as they were submerged in their watery grave.

Within only half an hour of ploughing into the rocks, the *Birkenhead* shared the same fate as the many other ships that had previously been wrecked off Danger Point. Some men were rescued by a schooner and others managed to swim ashore but at least 445 soldiers and sailors died, including the ship's captain, Robert Salmond.

There's some talk that Salmond was the very man who got the ill-fated *Birkenhead* into trouble in the first place. For starters, he had been sailing much too close to the shore and, secondly, he made a serious mistake by trying to reverse the stricken vessel off the rock – thus hastening its break up. But in the end, Robert Salmond, like Robert Stanford, got his corner of South Africa and today the Salmondsdam Nature Reserve bears his name.

Mariana's and Birkenhead Brewery

You shouldn't pass anywhere near Stanford without stopping at Mariana's at Owl's Barn Deli and Bistro in Du Toit Street. It's a deli-cum-restaurant run by the formidable Mariana and Peter Esterhuizen, who moved to Stanford from Cape Town in 1986. The Esterhuizens started their own organic vegetable garden that soon began producing too much for home consumption. This prompted the couple to start selling their wares at the market at the Old Harbour in Hermanus. They ran a stall at that market for 12 years and over time added deli goods such as home-made pasta, breads, jams, pickles and mayonnaise to the garden produce.

'We outgrew the market stall and decided to turn the Owl's Barn (previously self-catering accommodation) into a home deli with a few chairs and tables to serve the odd coffee or light lunch. We opened in January 2000 and soon realised that the demand far exceeded our expectations,' explains Mariana.

A visit to Stanford is not complete without a slice of Mariana's hearty Overberg chicken pie, made from a recipe handed down to her by her *Ouma* Franken, who grew up in the district (see opposite).

The Birkenhead Brewery is also a firm favourite and they make a variety of beers to suit every palate – from the sweetish Honey Blonde to the more serious Chocolate Stout. Some people go to extreme lengths to get at the brew and Andy Mitchell from the brewery has stories of thirsty workers decanting litres of beer into their gumboots. This is savoured throughout the day with the help of flexible rubber tubing, which they run from their boots through their overalls!

Mariana's chicken pie

1 whole, free-range chicken (forget about skinless, boneless bits, you lose too much flavour without the bones)
1 medium onion
4 bay leaves
10–12 whole cloves
1 cup water
¼ cup sago
2 dessert spoons brown sugar
3 dessert spoons apple cider vinegar or verjuice
salt
shortcrust or flaky pastry

Preheat oven to 180°C. Rinse chicken and place in oven-proof roasting pan with lid. Peel and quarter the onion and add this to the pan with bay leaves and cloves. Now pour in the water, cover the pan and cook for approximately 1½ hours. The cooking time will vary according to the size and age of the bird, but the end result should be fall-off-the-bone soft and succulent meat.

Pour the pan juices through a sieve and into a measuring jug. You will need 2 cups of juice, or, if the juice is too little, add boiling water until you have 2 cups of liquid. Pour this into a pan and add sago, brown sugar, apple cider vinegar or verjuice, and salt to taste. My *ouma* used home-made wine vinegar, but as this is not freely available anymore, I prefer the gentler acidity of cider vinegar or verjuice. Set this to a slow boil on the stove top and stir frequently, as sago can stick to the bottom of a pot and start burning the minute you turn your back.

In the meantime you can start preparing the meat. Remove all skin, bones and gristly bits and break the meat up into bite-sized pieces. (Don't be lazy now – use all those discarded bits to cook home-made stock.) Combine the meat and sago mixture and adjust flavouring to your liking. You now have a filling which you can turn into individual pies, one big pie or dainty cocktail pies. You can use either shortcrust or flaky pastry as a base, but traditionally the Overberg cooks took a lot of pride in their feather-light flaky pastry and used it at every opportunity.

We serve these pies with a salad of mixed organically grown leaves and home-cured olives, or roast vegetables and chilli jam according to the season. My *ouma* had never heard of salad greens such as rocket and mizuna, nor did she ever use home-cured olives, but I am sure she would approve of these modern accompaniments to her traditional pie.

ABOVE: The Klein River at Stanford offers excellent swimming, canoeing and bird-watching opportunities. TOP RIGHT: Stanford's quiet streets are a welcome change from the pace of the city. RIGHT: The open plain at Stanford was where wagons used to outspan in the early days. OPPOSITE TOP: The Klein River winds its way peacefully through the village. OPPOSITE MIDDLE: Stanford House offers guests quiet country hospitality. OPPOSITE FAR RIGHT: Old Man Lötter has been picking flowers in the area for decades.

STANFORD HOUS
Guest Lodge & Conference Centr
ENTRANCE AROUND
THE CORNER
TEL: 028 - 341 0300
FAX: 028 - 341 0522

Grootbos Private Nature Reserve

When the Lutzeyer brothers, Tertius and Michael, turned their family farm between Stanford and Gansbaai into a 1 700-hectare private nature reserve, they didn't just set out to create a luxury lodge for wealthy visitors keen to experience the good life. Rather, they set about finding a real way to contribute to the upliftment of the local community. And so, with the help of German funding, they launched Green Futures – a non-profit educational trust that teaches unemployed people from the local townships a trade in conservation and gardening, as well as life skills such as driving and how to run a small business.

Green Futures is a great partnership between the public and private sectors. Although the organisation receives overseas funding, within two years it needs to be self-sustainable and they're hoping to achieve this by starting a landscaping business and selling indigenous plants.

The Green Futures students have generated so much enthusiasm and support that they have even been given sponsored soccer kits from Manchester United. So, when the students aren't keeping an eye on the budding *Pelargonium betalinums* in the project's nursery, you will almost certainly find them practising their moves on the hotel's soccer field!

For visitors, there are guided walks/drives through the fynbos, a one-day tour (which is also open to people who are not staying at Grootbos) that includes an introduction to the fynbos, a trip to watch the whales and a walk along the nearby beach.

Interestingly, Grootbos has the largest remaining milkwood forest in the Western Cape.

Franskraal

The Strandveld Museum in Franskraal is a treasure trove. Built on a grassy patch just above the rocks, it contains a little of everything that tells of how things used to be before the facebrick houses with sleeping Mexican wall decorations made their mark along the shoreline.

The biggest gem of all, however, is Jan Fourie who, together with his wife SD, built and stocked the museum. Jan opens the museum when he's there and when he feels like it. He's *Oom* Attie's older brother (you'll meet *Oom* At in Napier, p121) and has the same crinkly eyes and throaty laugh. He also wears a beret at a jaunty angle but rides the waves instead of horses.

Once a schoolteacher, Jan is passionate about the sea and the men who made their living from it. His heart beats in time with the olden day guano collectors, seal hunters and fishermen from Dyer Island who pitted themselves against the elements and lived with the taste of salt on their lips. It was a tough life, but an honest one that had a brutal simplicity to it.

As a tribute to the men and the coast that shaped them, Jan wrote his book *Dawn at Dyer*. It's dedicated to Sampson Dyer, the man who first inhabited the island in 1806, and the Fourie's grandson, Ohlaf (see p87). The book is a tribute to the past and the future – and all the time in between. It starts with Jan's memories of holidays at the coast and, even though the details change from decade to decade, it captures an essence of holidays that every child should experience. In it he writes:

> *The team of oxen struggles through thick sand, the wagon wheels slicing track marks into the earth. Grandfather lashes out at the oxen with the long whip and eventually we arrive at the turn-off that leads down to the camping grounds. There, under burly milkwoods, the family tents are already standing pegged and anchored.*
>
> *Grandmother takes brown bread, the colour of straw, out of the dilapidated Dover stove that balances precariously on bricks. Ground coffee gets spooned into the coffee bag in the black kettle. After the customary greetings, exchanges of polite but useless information and family gossip, everyone gets coffee or orange syrup (depending on whether you are above or below the 'fleas in the stomach' age). Then we chased the guarry bushes covering the dune, to greet the ocean which we last saw a year ago.*
>
> *One of the island workers collects a batch of abalone and scrubs them clean. We are invited to stay for abalone fried in sheep fat! Aunty Maria squeezes lemon juice over the abalone.*
>
> *'You don't just tenderise abalone slightly,' she says, 'you beat it within an inch of its life ... then you fry it in a hot cast-iron pan. And then, you eat it, just like that!'*

Jan has plenty of memories worth listening to and there's nostalgia at every turn – you just need to make sure to pop by when he's there if you want to catch some of them.

OPPOSITE: Sand dunes at Die Plaat form part of the Walker Bay Reserve. TOP: *Oom* Jan runs Franskraal's Strandveld Museum. He is an excellent story-teller and a dab-hand at playing the accordion. Together with his wife, fondly known by everyone as SD, he has written a number of books about the area. ABOVE: Groot Hagelkraal Farm, at Pearly Beach in the Gansbaai area, is a Natural Heritage Site.

TOP: Buffeljagsbaai is beautiful and isolated – a place time seems to have forgotten (see text opposite). ABOVE, ABOVE RIGHT AND RIGHT: Die Dam campsite and caravan park is a real 'get away from it all' holiday spot. It's situated only a few metres from the crashing waves in Die Dam Conservation Area (see text opposite).

Island life

Dyer Island was first known as Isla da Fera (Island of Wild Animals) by Portuguese sailors during the fifteenth century. It lies about eight kilometres south of Franskraal and was named after Sampson Dyer, an American slave who was employed on the island in the early 1800s to club seals for their pelts, as well as bag the guano (or 'white gold') that was used for fertiliser. Jan Fourie writes:

> *One night, as he was sleeping peacefully in his hut, he was awoken with a shock by cannon fire from the direction of the island. Assuming that it was the provisions ship and thinking immediately of the 'fire water' which also made up part of his supplies, he kicked off his fur skin rug and dragged his little boat to the sea. Then, with fast powerful strokes he began rowing in the direction of the island. In the dim light of the sickle moon he saw the lights of a large American cargo ship on the northeastern side of the island. Hopelessly off course, the ship was anchored between the dangerous reefs. Sampson boarded the ship and found the ... crew in a panic-stricken state. After deliberation he asked the captain:*
>
> *'Have you got enough confidence to let me taken control of this ship?'*
>
> *'I have,' said the captain.*
>
> *'Fine and well,' Sampson answered him, 'with God's blessing everything will end well.'*

In what is regarded as masterful navigation, Sampson managed to sail the ship to safety and was rewarded with a guinea for his trouble.

For several decades in the 1800s a group of men lived a rough life on the island, harvesting pelts and bagging the guano for which Dyer Island was famous. According to old records, each year 2 000 to 4 000 seals were killed and the skins used for coats – especially for soldiers going off to war. The demand decreased after World War II and finally came to an end in 1984.

Another old name associated with Dyer Island was Black Sophie, the madam of a brothel in Cape Town. When she heard that the men on the island had reached breaking point, she loaded two wagons with a group of 'her girls' and made the treacherous journey over Sir Lowry's Pass to set up camp at Kleinbaai. A rock there has been named in her honour!

Times have changed dramatically and scientists have recommended that Dyer Island be registered as a wetland of international importance because it is home to just over one percent of the global population of the threatened African black oystercatcher. The island has been described as one of the jewels in the crown of Cape Nature.

Buffeljagsbaai

Not too far from Gansbaai is Buffeljagsbaai (Buffalo Hunt Bay), a strangely intriguing place that seems caught between the encroaching twenty-first century and the ageless, restless sea. The settlement is known today for its excellent fishing and its wild beauty, and the name must come from a legendary time of brave men hunting buffalo over the open plains – running swift and fast and aiming clean and true.

The Buffeljags shacks used to be constructed almost entirely out of timber from ships wrecked along the coast and they had a quaint, inventive feel to them that was emphasised by the buoys, thick ropes and netting draped over rickety fences. Now there's the odd Wendy house, some brick structures and plenty of corrugated iron. The residents are still almost entirely Groenewalds and Swaams. The founding father of the community, old Samuel Groenewald, arrived here around 1900 and the Swaams are here because they married the Groenewald daughters decades ago. They're a motley crew. You would have to be to live in this barren stretch, which – until a couple of years ago – had no electricity or piped water. There's a taut feistiness to the men, a glint bred through generations of coping with life on the outer edge.

'We are all poachers,' somebody volunteers with little prodding. 'What else are we meant to do? There are no more fish and the government has taken away our fishing permits because they say the stocks won't last. But all I know how to do is fish and dive for abalone. I grew up on the sea. Getting abalone is easy. They're right there,' he says, gesturing to the sea. 'In our back garden, so to speak. Men, women, children – it doesn't matter. You do what you have to do.'

What's the best way to cook perlemoen?

'You *sommer* make a fire and then put them on the coals.'

How do you know when they are done?

There's no answer for such a stupid question. If you've lived by the sea all your life and eat perlemoen every day, you just know.

Die Dam

For some families, Die Dam campsite and caravan park is an institution – their end-of-year bolthole where they go every summer to unwind. It's situated in Die Dam Conservation Area, which covers the unspoilt coastline between Quoin Point and Cape Agulhas, and is known for its snorkelling, angling and diving opportunities. The area is also home to a variety of aquatic birds, as well as a small colony of Cape fur seals.

At the resort itself, there's nothing quite as satisfying as finding the perfect spot for your umbrella, squeaking open a deck chair and settling down with a good book. For children, the possibilities are endless: days spent in swimming cozzies building sandcastles and eating ice-cream.

'All I know how to do is fish and dive for abalone ...'

Favourites

You can't leave the area without ...

- Eating at Mariana's restaurant in Stanford after admiring their organic vegetable garden. If the Gruyère soufflé is on the menu, don't hesitate – it's the closest thing to heaven you're going to eat for a long time. If it's not, bad luck, but you'll find something else just as good (see p80).
- Bird-watching by boat on the Klein River.
- Stocking up on the very best award-winning cheeses from the Klein River Cheese Factory and shop.
- Raising a glass of Birkenhead's brew to all those men and women who have lost their lives along this treacherous coastline (see p80).
- Scouring the rocky shoreline for pretty *alikreukel* and perlemoen shells to decorate your garden path.
- Doing a day tour at Grootbos Nature Reserve, where you'll learn about local fynbos, do a coastal walk and enjoy at delicious meal at the luxury hotel (see p84).
- Visiting Jan Fourie at his Strandveld Museum in Franskraal. Find a comfortable spot – there's usually a seal skin draped over a *bankie* – and ask him to play his accordion for you (see p85).
- Going whale watching with the legendary treasure hunter and conservationist, Wilfred Chivell, who takes tourists to Dyer Island. You can find him at the Great White House in Kleinbaai.
- Taking a leisurely drive through some of the prettiest countryside where you can stand on top of a hill covered with fynbos and look across towards the sea.

ABOVE: It's possible to buy fish straight from the ocean from the fish shop at Gansbaai Harbour. RIGHT AND TOP RIGHT: Country scenes from the tiny village of Stanford, which has a permanent population of around 3 000 residents (see p80). OPPOSITE TOP: Sunset at Uilkraalsmond Reserve, Pearly Beach. OPPOSITE BOTTOM: Holiday homes at De Kelders perch on the cliff high above the ocean. The hamlet's name means 'The Cellars'. FAR RIGHT: Stanford's pretty gardens and historic buildings can be appreciated on a walking tour. The core of the village is a conservation area.

STOP

Contact numbers

Stanford Tourism: 028-341-0340
Gansbaai, De Kelders, Franskraal, Uilkraalsmond and Pearly Beach Tourism: 028-384-1439

African Queen River Cruises: 082-732-1284
Birkenhead Brewery: 028-341-0183
Duiwelsgat hiking trail (De Kelders): 028-384-1439
Dyer Island Cruises (shark and whale watching): 082-801-8014 or 083-402-8541
Klein River Boat Cruises/Hire: 082-353-0588
Klein River Cheese: 028-341-0693
Mariana's at Owl's Barn Deli and Bistro: 028-341-0272
Salmondsdam Nature Reserve: 028-314-0062. Bookings on 028-425-5020
Shark diving trips: 028-384-1439
Strandveld Museum (Franskraal): By appointment only. 028-388-0218 or 082-255-8509

Where to stay
www.overberginfo.com
Blue Gum Country Estate (Stanford): 028-341-0116
Die Dam Camping and Angling Resort: 028-482-1710
Fair Hill Country House (Stanford): 028-341-0230
Grootbos Private Nature Reserve (Stanford): 028-384-0381
Syringa Stud Farm (Stanford): 082-450-3970
The Great White House (Gansbaai): 028-384-3273

TOP LEFT: Blue Gum Country Estate is a luxurious getaway that's run by Nic and Nicole Drupper, who made their name at the well-known Bartholomeus Klip Lodge. TOP RIGHT: Mariana's Deli and Bistro, Stanford, has a fantastic organic vegetable garden that's well worth exploring (see p80). RIGHT: Franskraal at Christmas time. OPPOSITE TOP LEFT: Stanford Trading Post has a great collection of enamel ware, old plates and collectibles that are ideal for your holiday home – or good to take back with you as a reminder of life in the country. OPPOSITE TOP RIGHT: Milkwood forest, Die Dam (see p87). OPPOSITE BOTTOM: The shifting sands at Die Plaat in the Walker Bay Reserve create remarkable patterns that change in an instant.

Wind, Sun & Sand

ARNISTON, STRUISBAAI and L'AGULHAS

TM 564

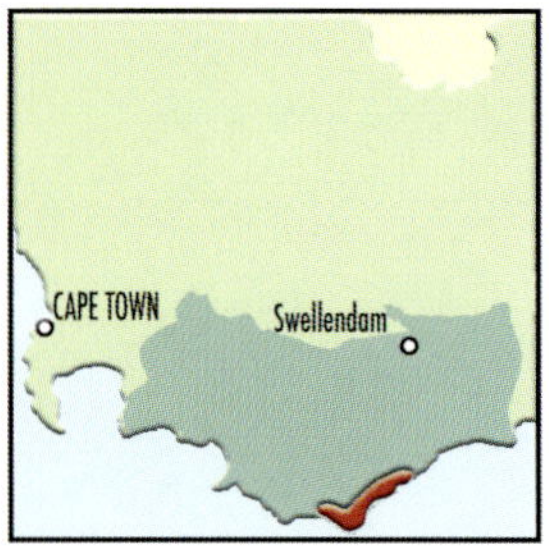

Who needs the Aegean when you've got the turquoise waters and pristine beaches of Arniston, Struisbaai and L'Agulhas? It's hardly surprising that this is one of the best-loved holiday destinations on the South African coastline. There are towering white sand dunes, great beaches for early morning walks with your sand-coated dogs, an endless choice of perfect swimming spots, fantastic fishing areas where all you'll see is a 'bamboo forest' of rods, and some memorable eating and drinking hang-outs.

Blown away in Arniston

This is the Arniston you've come to know and love. But she is something of a temperamental prima donna – just when you've got used to pulling on your costume first thing in the morning and taking your boogie board down to the beach, the wind arrives and *klaps* and howls until you've had more than enough of the sand in your ears and knots in your hair! There's even a local song that goes something like this:

Kassiesbaai is 'n lekker baai
Daar waar die suidoos so lekker waai
Hy waai my hier
En hy waai my daar
Hy waai my hare sommer deurmekaar
Die vis is volop
En die vleis is skaars
Daarom is die manne almal hengelaars

That's the thing about this coast – there are no half measures: it's either wild and stormy or perfectly blissful and the next best thing to heaven. And these extremes have shaped the people who live here. These are men who breathe in time with the tides and can't sleep without the sound of the restless ocean.

A town with three names

Arniston is named after the *HMS Arniston*, a British government troop ship that ran into trouble in 1815 on a voyage from Ceylon back to the Cape. The ship was carrying over 300 people – sailors, wounded soldiers, women and children – and, when the ship struck the Agulhas reef during heavy weather, they didn't stand a chance. Only a carpenter's mate and five sailors made it to shore, where they survived on shellfish until they were found by a farmer's son two weeks later.

A small community developed at Kassiesbaai shortly after the *Arniston* ran aground and the bay is named after the *kassies* or cases that washed ashore from the many vessels that ended belly-up on the reefs. The bodies from the *Arniston* were buried in groups of ten in the dunes north of Kassiesbaai and goods salvaged from the wreck were offered for sale by public auction two months later.

Arniston has always been a bit schizophrenic – which town with three names wouldn't be? Depending on who you meet, the village is either Arniston, Waenhuiskrans (Wagon House Cliff – after the famous cave that can be reached on foot at low tide) or Kassiesbaai, or a combination of all of these. Just as the names are different, so, too, are the communities that make up the town. There are the wealthy holiday-makers and retirees in the newer township, and the resident fisher community in the historic cottages in Kassiesbaai – a National Heritage Site.

The one thing that used to pull these two groups together was the shoals of yellowtail, Cape salmon and red steenbras that moved up and down the coast. That's all changed in recent years, though. Foreign fishing trawlers are hauling out enormous catches on their long lines, leaving the smaller boats and local fishermen who fish closer to the shore with extremely slim pickings.

Annelie Farao is just one of the women in Kassiesbaai who are battling to make ends meet. There are no men in the house and she observes that life is hard. The fish are scarce and getting scarcer by the day. When the wind blows the boats can't go out and there's no chance of fish for supper. On days like these, the men of the village search for *alikreukel* and octopus in the rocks in front of the town, but they don't always find anything. Sending your children to school on dry bread is no good, she says, but that's what they often have to do. Annelie does piecework in the village but it's seasonal and hardly enough to get by on. The house belonged to her parents and she's been there all her life.

It's difficult to marry this picture of simple fishing folk wanting to make an honest living out of the sea with the stories about poachers and drug runners that abound in the area. It's very hard to know which of these approximate the truth and which have moved out of reality into the realm of

urban myth. According to one Arniston resident, a local youth made 97 000 rand in a week through perlemoen poaching – he was just 18 years old.

However, come Sunday morning and it's easy to forget these rumours and harsh realities. The whitewashed church in Waenhuiskrans is filled with children in their Sunday best. The delicate lace curtains hanging in the simple building are decorated, quite appropriately, with a sail boat motif – a calm boat on a still sea – and the girls look like beautiful exotic flowers dressed in their pretty dresses made up of layers of lime green and mauve chiffon and shiny ribbons.

Waenhuiskrans's Hemingway-figure

Bob Harman, who owns the local café, is a true Arniston institution. He's a funny old chap and, depending on who you're talking to, he is either a lovable eccentric or an impossible old codger. Bob is a typical Hemingway figure: gruff, straight-talking and a man's man with a keen eye for the girls. His fingers are caught in an arthritic grasp that looks perfectly poised to hold a fishing rod – an old one, mind you, 'and none of this fancy, expensive graphite nonsense that costs the yuppies a couple of grand a shot.' He's had an extremely colourful life that could fill many books, and there's a quirkiness about him that few people would deny.

PREVIOUS SPREAD: De Mond Nature Reserve and other scenes from the region. THIS PAGE TOP: Arniston's picturesque harbour and fishing boats are among the area's main attractions. LEFT AND ABOVE: Twirly ice creams and starfish discovered in rock pools are the perfect images of summer holidays spent at the coast.

NERENJA
MARY-ANN
BR75XLT8

Bob's business card has a picture of him as a good-looking young man in red bathing shorts holding up a fish that's nearly as big as he is. It was a 67-pound leerie he caught back in the good old days. The card says: 'Bob: Fishing since 1933. Cooking since 1960.' As far as Bob is concerned, that statement pretty much sums up his life. He's fished and he's cooked. And he plans to carry on doing both these for as long as possible. He's also been living in the area for over 40 years and knows it like the back of his hand.

Bob is not exactly a conspiracy theorist but he definitely holds the previous government responsible for a series of decisions that were made to benefit a few of the inner circle. After all, he once lived happily at Skipskop – just up the coast from Arniston. That was before the Armscor representatives took away people's land in the early 1980s and made the area into a Missile Test Range known more formally as the Overberg Toetsbaan. Why, Bob wants to know with increasing exasperation, would the government take away a prime coastal area for a test range when there are tracts of unattractive land they could have appropriated instead of stealing the southern jewel of tourism?

'Skipskop was paradise,' says Bob wistfully. 'This is where the famous Bredasdorp oysters came from. They were big buggers and the man who had the concession supplied some of the restaurants in Cape Town with them. My fiancée and I discovered the area by chance,' he goes on to explain. 'This was at the end of the 1950s and there was hardly anything happening out here. I ended up buying two seafront plots in Struisbaai for 350 rand each. Now you can't get anything for under a million on the seafront.

Bob feels just as strongly about the subject of fishing quotas. He isn't the only one, of course. This isn't a problem specific to the area, but rather affects all of the fishermen and fisherwomen along the Overstrand. Spend time in any bar, and before long, talk will turn to fishing quotas and permits.

There are no fish left in these waters, says Bob, because the industry is unregulated. The *skelms* – both locals and foreigners – are responsible for the wholesale plunder and they have no regard for the legacy they'll leave behind. He remembers selling huge yellowtail for five rand each. Now fish are being caught and shipped out to the Far East for sushi, and a big bluefin tuna will net you at least 30 000 rand in Tokyo.

Bob still goes fishing every day if the weather's any good but his old fishing pals are dwindling. The legendary Jock Dichmont died a couple of years back and that was a huge loss. He was one of Arniston's favourite sons and a tribute to him hangs in the Arniston Hotel. Jock was a great personality and, amongst other things, he is remembered for his involvement in the salvage

These are men who eat, sleep and breathe fish talk.

PREVIOUS SPREAD LEFT: Arniston's fishing boats are stranded in the harbour on windy days. PREVIOUS OPPOSITE TOP LEFT: Craggy rocks, like those found at Struispunt, define this rugged shoreline. PREVIOUS OPPOSITE TOP RIGHT: A climb up the sand dunes gives stunning views of the unspoilt beach. PREVIOUS BOTTOM LEFT: The dunes change position regularly – there's little in this area that the wind can't move. PREVIOUS BOTTOM RIGHT: Thousands of smooth, flat rocks cover parts of the beach – and the clicking sound made as the waves roll over them is mesmerising. THIS SPREAD RIGHT: Bob Harman with his daughter Roanne at the Arniston Café. FAR RIGHT: Bob in his heyday with a whopping fish that weighed nearly as much as he did. OPPOSITE TOP: On days when the boats can't go out, the men search for food in the rock pools (see p94). OPPOSITE LEFT: Battling the wind and waves to get the boat off the slipway. OPPOSITE MIDDLE: The quaint fishing village of Kassiesbaai perches on the cliff above the harbour at Arniston. OPPOSITE RIGHT: The catch of the day is red roman – good to eat no matter how you prepare it.

B49
49
UITEINDELIK

team that dived for treasure off the wreck of the *Merestein* in the early 1970s. The *Merestein*, which went down in April 1702, was carrying a cargo of rare coins, which was why there was so much excitement surrounding the salvage operations.

Like Jock, Bob and his compatriots are men who eat, sleep and breathe fish talk. They can tell you the pros and cons of grab sinkers versus bottle sinkers, have favourite coffee grinder reels that they've inherited from friends or family, and most have scars on their hands from 'the huge shark that whipped my butt one legendary Sunday 20 years ago.'

People like these feel passionate about this coastline because the stakes are so high – where else do you get such exceptional fishing and swimming? It's a paradise everyone wants to defend against too much change.

Great Arniston institutions

Die Waenhuis (The Wagon House) is as much a part of Arniston as its owner, Bob. Like most great places, it had a previous life before it became a restaurant. It was a cowshed and a storeroom, piled high with junk and detritus. 'Organic kitsch' is how the décor been described. Who else could get away with a talking fish and a laughing lobster on the bar counter and a dated poster of a busty cyclist, together with red-and-white checked tablecloths?

Auntie Nellie Murtz has been cooking with Bob for over 20 years and he prides himself on having a fantastic local team from Kassiesbaai – all of whom have been working with him for decades. Everyone has their favourite dishes that they order time and again from a menu that is so retro that it's almost

ABOVE: Lillian Newman at the Kassiesbaai Craft Centre, where visitors can buy crafts created by the residents, or treat themselves to a delicious traditional meal. RIGHT AND OPPOSITE TOP, BOTTOM LEFT AND CENTRE: Impressions and people of Kassiesbaai – a National Heritage Site named after the *kassies*, or cases, that washed ashore from the many ships wrecked in these treacherous waters. OPPOSITE BOTTOM RIGHT: Arniston's famous cave can be visited on foot at low tide. OVERLEAF TOP AND BOTTOM: You can't leave the area without trying Aunt Nellie's famous s*oetpatats*, or the Arniston Hotel's seafood bouillabaisse. OVERLEAF OPPOSITE: De Mond Reserve, between Struisbaai and Arniston, on a quiet day.

fashionable again. On the right is one of Aunt Nellie's most famous recipes for *soetpatats*. Yes, Napier, is known as the *soetpatat* capital of South Africa (see p120), but it's just up the road from Arniston and Nellie's dish is so popular that people order huge servings to take back to Cape Town with them when their holiday comes to an end.

A word of caution, however: there's no guarantee that this dish will taste as brilliant when you're back home working nine to five as it does when Aunt Nellie makes it. There's something about getting up at dawn to go fishing that sharpens the appetite and makes everything taste exceptional. But, when you're starting to hanker for sand between your toes and the zing of the fishing line when a fish bites, give this recipe your best shot.

For a taste of the real Waenhuiskrans, also be sure to visit the Kassiesbaai Craft Centre that's situated in the village and has a great view over the village and ocean. You will be able to buy craftwork done by the women (and a few men) and, if you order beforehand, they'll serve you a traditional meal with all the trappings. There's home-baked bread, green bean *bredie*, the freshest fish, an assortment of salads and malva pudding and custard to finish off a perfect meal.

Another great Arniston institution is the Arniston Hotel – a well-known watering spot perfect for sundowners on the terrace, or a leisurely lunch with lots of chilled wine while overlooking the ocean just 100 metres away.

The hotel opened in the 1930s and was a favourite with local fishermen but over the decades this has changed and it's now a more up-market getaway attracting regular guests from both locally and abroad. Even if you're not staying in one of their exquisite sea-facing rooms, the dining room is certainly worth a visit. Although the menu changes regularly, the combination of Cape Malay flavours with more cosmopolitan influences is one of the hotel's trademarks (see recipe below).

Auntie Nellie's *soetpatats*

- 2 tbsps butter
- 2½ cups sugar
- 1 cup water
- 1 tbsp custard powder dissolved in ½ cup water
- 2 kg sweet potatoes
- 1 piece ginger
- 3 pieces cinnamon

Caramelise the butter and 1½ cups sugar. Add 1 cup water and stir till it forms a brown sauce. Add *patats* with the remaining cup of sugar, ginger and cinnamon and cook for 45 minutes. The *patats* must still be firm. Add custard mixture and stir for 10 minutes, then leave to simmer. After 45 minutes switch off the stove and leave to stand for 20 minutes before serving. Serve with freshly grilled kabeljou and salad. Or don't bother with any of those and just go for the *patats*!

Arniston Hotel's bouillabaisse

- 1 chopped onion
- 2½ t grated ginger
- 2½ t chopped garlic
- 5 chopped bananas
- 5 t curry powder
- 1¼ litres fish stock or mussel stock
- 1¼ litres each milk & cream
- salt & pepper to taste
- 4 mussels
- 2 large prawns in shell
- 8 small prawns without shell
- 6 calamari tubes
- 200 g geelbek cut in 3
- 1 or 2 lemons

Fry onions, ginger, garlic, bananas and curry powder. Add fish or mussel stock, milk, cream and add the seasoning. Reduce to half. Add all the seafood ingredients. Cook with sauce, add freshly squeezed lemon juice and check seasoning. Serve with a garlic-rubbed home-made *potbrood* and lemon halves.

TOP: Weekend traffic – everyone goes fishing at Struisbaai's harbour! ABOVE AND RIGHT: There are some outstanding swimming and boating opportunities in the turquoise waters of Struisbaai. OPPOSITE: Welcome to the southernmost tip of Africa and Cape L'Agulhas. This is where the two oceans – the warm Indian and icy Atlantic – meet. The stretch of coast is known, very ominously, as the Graveyard of Ships (see p106).

Struisbaai

Struisbaai is a fishing village that has the longest stretch of pristine coastline in the southern hemisphere. It's 14 kilometres of seaside paradise and great for swimming, boating and fishing. There's some debate about how the town got its name – some think it was named after the *vogelstruise* (ostriches) found in the area, while others believe it might have been to do with the houses that were built out of straw (*struis*) bales. There's another theory that says it was named after the size of its beach, as *struis* is an old Dutch word for 'huge'.

What's not in debate is just why people come here every year. You only have to look at *bakkies* that are specially modified to carry at least ten fishing rods safely if you want to get an idea of what motivates these *ouens*. And look around – you'll see boats named *Gooi Los* and houses called Knot 4 Sail. Struisbaai also made headlines in the 1990s when they advertised a whale braai. Of course this went down a treat with the environmentally minded, but it does give insight into the personality of the town.

At the entrance to Struisbaai are the pretty historical Hotagterklip fishermen's cottages. They've been declared national monuments and are a testimony to the old folks who first eked out a living from the sea. The pretty thatched church is also an historic monument.

Each year, Struisbaai holds its famous *Geelstert Fees* in honour of the mighty yellowtail that has (mostly) men up first thing in the morning in its pursuit. On the back page of a recent edition of the *Suidernuus*, the local newspaper, there's a grainy photo of Johan Claasen, a fisherman on the Struisbaai vessel the *Sangoma*, who managed to catch a yellowtail weighing a record 23.8 kilograms on the 19-kilometre bank only a few years back.

De Mond Nature Reserve

The unspoilt De Mond Nature Reserve lies at the mouth of the Heuningnes River between the villages of Arniston and Struisbaai. The reserve is home to the highly-threatened Damara tern (*Sterna balaenarum*), which has established a breeding colony on the pebble beds between the dune fields.

De Mond has been earmarked by the Ramsar Convention – an inter-governmental treaty on the conservation of wetlands – as a wetland of international importance, and therefore as worthy of continued protection. There's plenty to do in the reserve. Birding is top of the list but the fishing is also excellent and you'll pit your wits against grunter, steenbras, leervis, elf, cob, springer and striped harder.

There's also the seven-kilometre Sterna Trail, which takes between two and three hours to hike. This is a circular route that takes walkers through spectacular dune milkwood thickets, and limestone and dune fynbos. You can also walk from De Mond to Arniston along the coast, passing Waenhuiskrans Cave, nearby fish traps (see overleaf) and Khoisan middens along the way.

Ancient fishing traps

Today's *manne* with their modified 4x4s and expensive fishing rods are by no means the first fishermen to stake their claim along this coast. Thousands of years ago, the Khoekhoen and San built extensive tidal fishing traps or *vywers* to capture the bounty from the sea.

The design is ingenious – loose stones were piled up to create dams that filled up when the tide came in and then left the fish stranded as it receded. It's hard to put an exact date on when these fish traps were established but, next time you go puddle-hopping looking for anemones, limpets and starfish, keep in mind that over 2 000 years ago people were doing the same thing. Look out for fish traps at Rasperpunt, Kruismansbaai, Pearly Beach, Struisbaai and Arniston.

L'Agulhas

It's not for nothing that the stretch of coast around the southernmost tip of Africa is known as the 'Graveyard of Ships'. You only have to look at the area names near Struisbaai and L'Agulhas to get a sense of how dangerous these waters are. There's Schoonberg Bay after a Dutch Indiaman wrecked in 1722, St Mungo Point after a barque that came to grief in 1844 and Northumberland Point after an English Indiaman that went down in 1838.

It's the potent combination of strong winds, wild seas and treacherous undercurrents that makes this coast so difficult to navigate – as more than 120 ships, including the *HMS Arniston* (see p94), have discovered to their peril. The fact that the early compasses also went haywire around Cape L'Agulhas didn't help the help the mariners of old much either.

Early Portuguese sailors called this cape 'Cabo das Agulhas', which means the Cape of Needles, as an ironic observation that, on passing this point, their compass needles showed no real deviation between true and magnetic north. Given that this was well before the age of instantaneous communication, this discovery came far too late for many.

The old public notices advertising the auctions of the goods from ships wrecked along the coast make for intriguing reading. They speak of faraway lands, exotic cargos and an entirely different world from the big container ships that

TOP: L'Agulhas National Park has a plant species richness equalling that of tropical rainforests. ABOVE: Khoekhoen fish traps were designed to catch fish as the tides came in and then receded. RIGHT: A cairn marks the spot where the two oceans meet. OPPOSITE: The view from the Agulhas Lighthouse includes the replica of a masthead that can be seen in the Bredasdorp Shipwreck Museum.

L'Agulhas – Africa's southernmost point

- Latitude 34°49'58" south and longitude 20°00'12" east
- 6 135 kilometres from the South Pole
- 3 882 kilometres from the North Pole
- 9 797 kilometres from London.

now ply the oceans. Here's a taste of what was on offer. From the wreck of the *Elizabeth A. Oliver* interested parties could buy nine bales of straw hats and 400 packets of superior green tea. The *Minnie* offered up 2 000 Hogshead staves, eight barrels of biscuits, four cases of Sago & Blue and six fox traps. The *Borderer* was laden at Penang for London and her salvaged cargo consisted of rum, tin, rattans, pepper, hides, sugar and tapioca. From the *Osmond* there was only one case of ostrich feathers.

The fascinating Shipwreck Museum in Bredasdorp is worth a few hours of browsing and you'll soon lose yourself in imagining what life on board some of these ships must have been like. One of the most exotic ships – and reportedly the richest – to run aground in these waters was the *Nossa Senhora De Los Milagros*. The ship was bound for Europe from the East with three Siamese mandarins who were on their way to pay homage to the kings of Portugal and France.

When the ship sank in 1686, there were only a few survivors who embarked on a harrowing walk from L'Agulhas to the Castle of Good Hope in the Cape. The records in the National Archives show that the ship was carrying precious stones, jewels, porcelain, gold and silver – all gifts for the kings they never met. At the time of the wreck, the ship was plundered extensively and a large number of locals landed up in jail for their troubles.

L'Agulhas National Park

Don't be too quick to drive past the rugged coastline hugging the southernmost tip of Africa. It may be a bit rough around the edges but that's half its charm. This area is often referred to as the Agulhas Plain and forms part of the extensive L'Agulhas National Park. The park is of international significance because of its rich plant biodiversity, with species richness equalling that of tropical rainforests. Here are some figures to think about: The L'Agulhas National Park is home to approximately 2 000 species of indigenous plants, including 100 that are endemic to the area, and over 110 Red Data Book species.

If you're a keen bird watcher, the wetlands will hold an irresistible pull. Each year it's estimated that over 21 000 migrant and resident wetland birds pass through the area, and it won't be too long before you'll catch sight of the African black oystercatcher and Damara tern, while the Karoo robin and Cape bunting are amongst the smaller species.

The wetlands don't just attract thousands of birds, however. One of the park's gems is the Cape platanna frog. To be sure you don't miss it: the Cape platanna, or *Xenopus gilli*, is about the size of your thumb from snout to vent. It also has dark stripes on the back and a mottled stomach. Unfortunately, as development rapidly encroaches on the wetlands, this tiny creature is fast becoming one of the most endangered species in the world.

TOP: Boats in Struisbaai's harbour are moored for the moment, but are ever ready to ride the waves. ABOVE: Inside Arniston's cave – famous for supposedly being large enough for an ox wagon to turn around in. ABOVE MIDDLE: These small beach villages are ideal for children, as they can roam in safety with their holiday mates for hours on end. ABOVE RIGHT: An early morning walk on the beach at Arniston involves lots of tidal pool gazing. There are starfish, anemones and tiny darting fish to admire. RIGHT: Suiderstrand at L'Agulhas. OPPOSITE: It's little wonder that people fall in love with this stretch of coastline. There are the picture-perfect boats, the startlingly blue sea – and days of endless possibilities.

Favourites

You can't leave the area without ...

- Eating fresh fish and chips from one of the shops in Struisbaai while overlooking the ocean (see p104).
- Climbing to the top of the Cape Agulhas Lighthouse. Hold onto your hat if there's a stiff wind blowing, otherwise this is the last you'll see of it (see p106).
- Buying one of Raymond Lawrence's paintings of the fishermen's cottages that have made this area famous. He sells his paintings from his house in Waenhuiskrans village and at local B&Bs and the Arniston Hotel.
- Getting all nostalgic looking at the old fishing photographs tacked up in the Arniston Café.
- Visiting the famous Waenhuiskrans Cave. It's so named because it's supposedly large enough to house a wagon and span of oxen.
- Stopping by the Kassiesbaai Craft Centre. Be sure to chat to Lillian or Maria – they'll be able to fill you in on all the news from the village (see p102).
- Missing a tortoise that is making its torturous trek across the tarmac.
- Going birding at Soetendalsvlei, southern Africa's largest natural body of fresh water. The shoreline and grasslands around the vlei host a variety of bird and animal species.
- Getting up before dawn to go fishing with your mates. You'll be spoilt for choice: De Mond, Dassies Gat and Die Mass are just a few of the places you can choose from.

ABOVE: Arniston's famous towering dunes.
RIGHT TOP: Sunset at Arniston Point.
RIGHT MIDDLE: The cosy Arniston Hotel and the fishing village of Kassiesbaai have uninterrupted views of Arniston Bay and the ocean beyond.
RIGHT AND OPPOSITE LEFT AND RIGHT: Dense milkwood thickets meet the beaches at De Mond Nature Reserve, which is great for hiking enthusiasts (see p104). The Heuningnes Estuary at De Mond is home to 100 bird species and is a popular angling spot.

Contact numbers

Suidpunt Tourism (Arniston, Struisbaai, Agulhas): 028-424-2584
Agulhas National Park (also for Agulhas Lighthouse): 028-435-6078
Arniston Centre (Arniston Café and Die Waenhuis): 028-445-9797
De Mond Nature Reserve: 028-424-2170
Kassiesbaai Crafts Centre: 028-445-9760
Rusvic Great White Charters (Struisbaai): 028-435-6221

Where to stay

www.overberginfo.com
Agulhas Country Lodge: 028-435-7650
Arniston Hotel: 028-445-9000
Arniston Lodge: 028-445-9175
Arniston Seaside Cottages: 028-445-9772
Blue Whale B&B: (Struisbaai) 028-435-6554
Die Herberg (Arniston): 028-445-9240
Pride of Africa Lodge (Bredasdorp): 028-435-6903

Blue, Green & Gold

CALEDON,
NAPIER,
BREDASDORP
ELIM
BAARDSKEERDERSBOS
and
WOLVENGAT

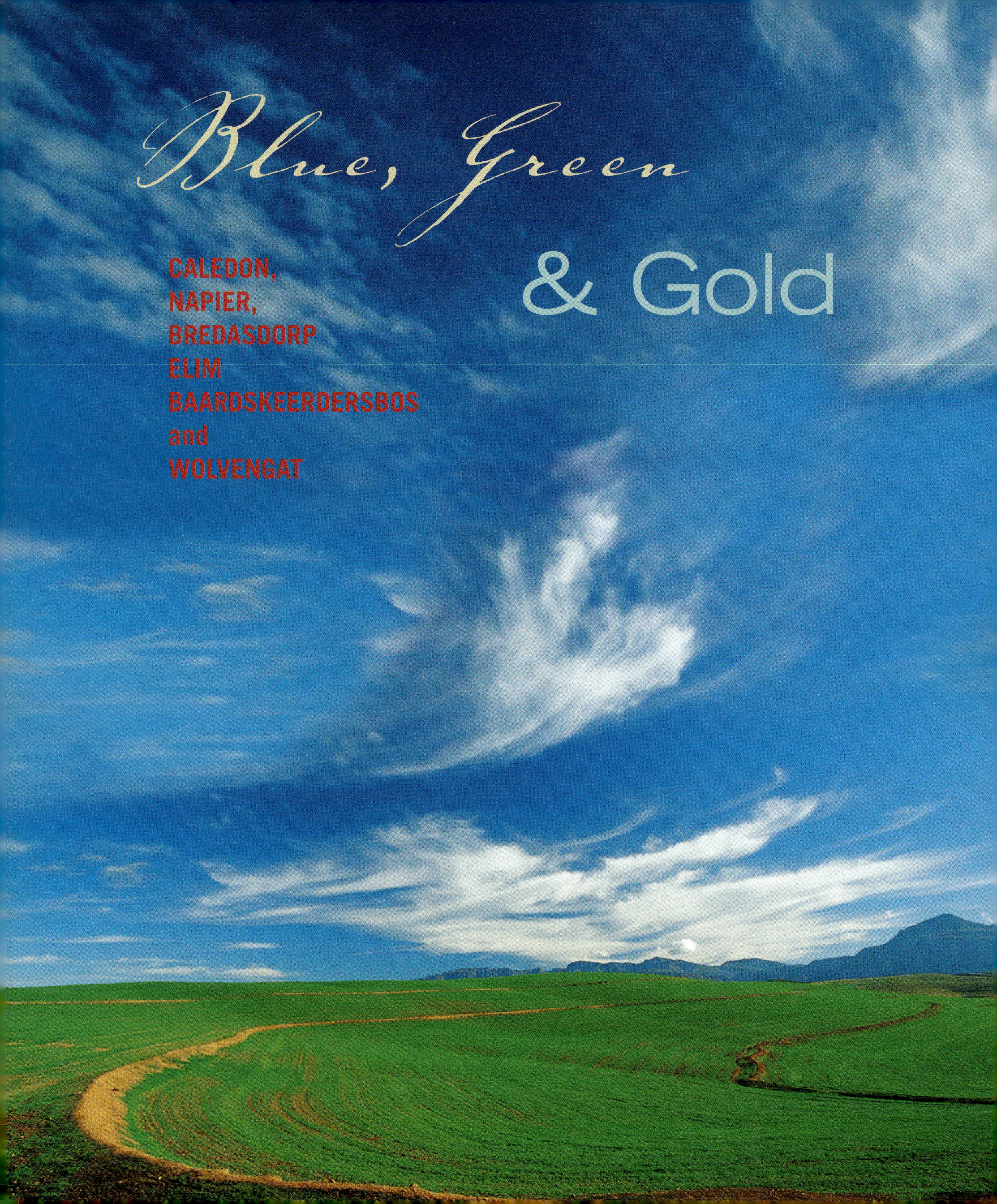

CAFE
Hierdie Besigheid
AKSIE TEEN
This Bussiness Supports
FIGHT AGAINST

Welcome to Big Sky Country where rolling fields of green or gold unfold before you and you'll find all the space you need to breathe. The land between the towering mountains and the sea is known as the rûens, or ruggens, because it looks like the undulating rise and fall of a person's back. In spring, the ruggens are transformed by a blanket of yellow canola flowers, forming a breathtaking contrast against the crisp blue of the sky.

The charm of Caledon

Caledon is the capital of the Overberg and it's no surprise that it grew where it did: the hot and cold mineral springs that bubble out at the base of the Klein Swartberg are impossible to resist. Long before white settlers trekked into the Overberg, local indigenous tribes also enjoyed the curative powers of the waters. By the early 1700s, however, white settlers had claimed the springs as their own and in 1710 Ferdinand Appel was granted 10 hectares at the hot springs and was instructed to build accommodation for visitors. A century later, in 1810, a village had grown on the farm Swartberg and was renamed after the Earl of Caledon three years later.

Caledon developed slowly in the early years as it served a poor farming community and, despite the proximity of the springs, water in the village was scare. By the 1840s, however, the introduction of the wool-producing merino sheep changed the fortunes of farmers in the Overberg and the region became one of the most prosperous in the Colony (see p124). Today the Caledon/Napier/Bredasdorp stretch is one of South Africa's richest agricultural areas, contributing hundreds of thousands of rands to the economy each year.

Unlike the holiday towns along the coast, the atmosphere inland is very different. These are hard-working towns and they have a gravitas their fun-loving coastal cousins lack. Here the farming co-op has pride of place in the main street and hugely expensive green and gold tractors take up lots of window space. Each year tons of wheat, oats and barley are produced on isolated farms that stretch as far as the eye can see. Onions, potatoes, sheep and horses also thrive here, and many family fortunes have been founded on these soils.

Get out your calculators – when it comes to quantifying just how much agricultural produce comes from this region, your head is likely to spin. Johan Lusse from CRK Agriculture Limited gives a rundown: 'On average our area produces 85 000 tons of wheat, around 52 000 tons of barley, 7 000 tons of oats and about 12 000 tons of canola. There are approximately 300 000 sheep in the area and they produce 1.2-million kilograms of wool and 3.4-million kilograms of meat. We also produce 4.8-million litres of milk each year.'

Because the scenery is so breathtaking, chances are you're going to want to do as much exploring as possible. There are a number of 4x4 routes in the area, and you'll be able to test your driving skills on the Voorhoede Route, which takes you to the top of the Klein Swartberg and is rated about three out of ten in terms of difficulty.

If you prefer to stretch your legs, pay the Caledon Nature Reserve and Wild Flower Garden a visit. Also known as Victoria Park, the reserve was established in 1899 and is a major drawcard in the area. It extends across over 200 hectares of the Swartberg, 56 hectares of which have been beautifully landscaped with indigenous flora. There's also a 10-kilometre walk that takes you through the reserve and to the famous rock known as The Window.

For insight into what life must have been like for the town's first citizens, pop in at the Caledon Museum – an original house furnished in the style of the late Victorian period (1870–1900). If you time your morning visit well, you might be lucky enough to sample some of the fresh bread that is still baked in the old woodstove and sold to the public.

Boontjieskraal

Boontjieskraal is one of the oldest farms in the Overberg. Back in the late 1800s it was a landmark for anybody making the trip along the arduous Cape Wagon Route into the interior and its history is intricately linked with names like Hermanus Pieters (see p52) and other well-known South Africans. This is De Wet territory, after all, and General de Wet's father was born on the farm.

There's some debate about how Boontjieskraal (which translates very clumsily into something like 'Bean Enclosure') got its name. One possibility is that it was named after a local leader, Jan Boontjies. However, the great naturalist and early African explorer William Burchell mentioned in his book *Travels in the Interior of Southern Africa* that the farm was named after the small stones found in the Swart River that runs through the farm. The tiny, polished stones looked so much like beans that, legend has it, naming the area after the stones seemed like the logical thing to do.

Some like it hot

People have been enjoying the restorative waters of the Caledon hot springs for centuries – long before the Victorian bathhouse was built and it became a stylish destination for gentry from 'the Cape'. Old photos from the turn of the 20th century show a gracious sanatorium with dance halls, billiard tables, croquet lawns and library – the perfect place to recuperate after a nightmarish journey out from England. In 1904 reports published in Cape Town extolled the waters' healing properties and there was no shortage of takers. Unfortunately, the sanatorium burnt down in 1946 and took with it a part of Caledon's history and its cachet as a fashionable resort town. You can still take to the waters, though, and loll around in the beautiful Victorian baths or go for the full monty at the recently restored hotel and spa where you can get everything from mud wraps to invigorating massages.

PREVIOUS SPREAD: Caledon farmlands and other scenes from the region. THIS SPREAD TOP: Hot springs at the Caledon Spa and Casino. ABOVE: The Dassiesfontein Farmstall on the way to Caledon is a shopper's paradise, where you'll find Dover stoves, *bokkoms*, thick plaits of Overberg onions and hearty meals. RIGHT: The end of the school day means long afternoons of carefree fun to look forward to.

The farm has been in the De Wet family for generations and has passed from father to son so many times that the pepper trees lining the driveway to the homestead seem to whisper their names. Today, its caretakers are Doreza and Uwe Kersandt. Doreza is a De Wet who was born on Boontjieskraal and grew up there.

The homestead is full of family mementoes: old photos of bearded ancestors, stern-looking women who could plough a straight line and hundreds of trophies won at agricultural shows. The farm was, and still is, famous for its teams of mules, dairy cows and award-winning sheep.

At the entrance is a carpet with the family motto woven into it. It reads: *Solum Deo Confido*, which means 'Only In God We Trust'. Some people might argue that the family has been granted divine protection. Doreza says, 'All of us on Boontjieskraal have a lot to be thankful for, but we have always shared our blessings.'

There's plenty to be grateful for – 3 000 hectares of prime land and a sense of belonging and responsibility that only comes from having farmed the land for generations and knowing its every nook and cranny.

Standing at the highest point of the farm, you can see for miles. There's Babilonstoring in the distance, and the indigo peaks of the Sonderend Mountains. Blue cranes come and go in elegant flight and a light wind rustles the young green shoots of wheat that are pushing through the soil. The De Wet family seems to have found a slice of heaven on earth right here on Boontjieskraal.

Cape Snow

There's a wonderful photograph from Caledon in the early 1900s. It's of a little girl sitting in a wagon that's being pulled by two boys in matching navy uniforms. The children are obviously taking part in one of the local flower shows, and their mother is proudly standing by. What's so special about the wagon, however, is that every inch of it is covered in *sewejaartjies*, the Cape everlasting this area is famous for.

The botanical name is *Syncarpha vestita*, but these pretty, papery flowers are known by a number of other sobriquets. There's *strooiblommetjie*, *matras sewejaartjie*, *tontelblom* and Cape snow. But these flowers are most commonly known as *sewejaartjies* – so named because they only last for seven years.

When it comes to harvesting, the best time to pick them is when the sky is overcast and the flowers are closed. They're then dried in packing sheds before being shipped to various parts of the world for use in dried funeral wreaths and flower arrangements.

There are different versions of the following story, but one goes that newcomers to the district believed the area was haunted because they used to see wagons trundling by in the early morning mist piled high with what looked like coffins. They weren't coffins, of course, but rather the carefully packed *sewejaartjies* sewn into sacks ready for export.

PREVIOUS SPREAD LEFT PAGE, TOP LEFT: The Caledon area produces 85 000 tons of wheat a year (see p114). TOP RIGHT AND RIGHT PAGE, TOP: Farmlands on the *rûens* – the rolling Overberg countryside named for its resemblance to the curves of a person's back. These hilly formations are also known as ruggens. BOTTOM: An old photograph of Boontjieskraal taken in the mid-1900s (see p114). THIS SPREAD FAR LEFT: Canola fields near the Caledon Reserve are a brilliant green in winter time. LEFT: The same fields turn bright yellow in the spring and summer. OPPOSITE CLOCKWISE FROM TOP: *Sewejaartjies* on Drie Wolwehondenes farm near Caledon (see text above).

Napier Farm Stall & Restaurant

There's something about life in the country that sharpens the appetite and makes every meal a feast – whether it's sun-warmed tomatoes from your garden eaten on top of fresh bread with crunchy salt, or toast with cheese and green fig preserve.

This is home produce territory after all, and there's a farmstall on every corner. Be prepared to go home with so much that you'll have enough jam and preserves to last you for the next 10 years. Keep a look out for bottled guavas, jewel-coloured fig jam, chunks of watermelon preserve and creamy home-made feta cheese. Then there are the koeksisters, *buttermilk rusks, vetkoek and freshly baked bread you'd be crazy to pass up on.*

Napier Farm Stall makes a fabulous sweet potato muffin that is everything a muffin should be – spicy, nutty, rich and wholesome.

Soetpatat muffins

Makes six big muffins

2 eggs
1½ cups sugar
¾ cup oil
2 cups milk
½ t vanilla essence
1 cup very strong coffee
2 cups digestive bran
2 cups self-raising flour
2½ t bicarbonate of soda
1 cup grated raw sweet potato and apple

Cream the eggs and sugar, add oil, milk and vanilla. Add the coffee. Then add the rest of the ingredients. Store the mixture in the fridge for about 30 minutes.

Then bake for about 20 minutes at 180°C. Serve warm with butter and your morning cup of coffee. Now this is a civilised way to start your day ...

RIGHT: Napier is famous as the sweet potato capital of South Africa.
TOP RIGHT: Jars of preserves line the shelves of the Overberg farmstalls, reminding you of granny's pantry.
OPPOSITE LEFT AND RIGHT: The Napier Farm Stall & Restaurant serves hearty meals of fresh bread, salad and home-made pies. Follow this up with an irresistible juicy *koeksister* – or two!

Napier

Known as the *soetpatat* capital of the country, Napier was established in 1838 after two prominent country barons – Pieter van der Byl and Michiel van Breda – locked horns over where the Dutch Reformed Church for the growing community should be built. As both were stubborn old goats accustomed to getting their own way, neither was prepared to back down. The result was that two enormous churches were built only 16 kilometres apart at Napier and Bredasdorp. It's obvious whom Bredasdorp was named after (Van Breda was later the first mayor of Cape Town), but Van der Byl declined the privilege and wrote instead to Sir George Napier, Governor of the Cape, and asked for his permission to name the settlement after him.

Home truths reveal themselves pretty quickly in small towns where people have the time to talk. In Napier this homespun wisdom goes something like this: everyone in the town owns a horse (if they don't, they aren't really from Napier) and everyone has a story (you just have to stay still for long enough to let them tell it to you). And (bar a couple of farmers and country die-hards) just about everyone has done something else before coming to Napier. There's watercolour artist Alan Raubenheimer who now has a toy museum and makes steam boats (Rose's Art and Toy World); former garage owner and naval engineer Kevin Doveton who makes incredible cantering horse and steam engine whirligigs; and long-ago military man, Leon Visser, who

now fashions intricate chess sets. He also has an alter-ego he calls 'The Butler' who works in his wife's coffee shop – Napier All Sorts – when he's not showing people around his military museum or experimenting with molten lead.

There's a charm to villages like this that's hugely appealing. Follow a sign that says 'Quilting and home produce', and you'll come across a small-town phenomenon – a shop, an open door and an honesty box. The idea behind this madness is simple: if you want something and nobody's home, you're welcome to take it, but just write down your purchases and put your money in the box. Thank you very much.

There's also an earthy humour here that gives an insight into just how wacky South Africans really are. When a particularly skinny woman (clearly an import not raised on meat and three veggies) moved to the area and got stung by a bee she swelled up dramatically and within a couple of minutes was doing an excellent impression of a blimp. On her way to hospital she bumped into some overweight local *tannies* who took one look at her grossly swollen face and shrieked with laughter. 'Now you look like us,' they hooted.

For unique insight into the town, book yourself onto the popular walking tour called Footprints through Napier – a local guide will walk you past places of interest and tell you intriguing stories about the town and its inhabitants. Booking is through the Napier tourist information office (see p135).

Oom Attie

One person who has never been anywhere other than Napier and has never been anything else other than himself is Attie Fourie, mostly known as *Oom* Attie or even *Oom* At. He's a Napier old-timer and the salt-of-the-earth sort – a straight talker with little time for newfangled ideas and modern nonsense. With his beret set at a cheeky angle and a cigarette clamped between his fingers, here's a man who knows everything anyone needs to know about horses, donkey carts, fixing things and living simply.

Oom Attie lives out of town on a hill with a sweeping view. His brother, Wessel, lives in a cottage on the smallholding and it's packed with furniture antique dealers would give their eyeteeth to get their hands on. The Fourie family is obviously pretty exceptional as another brother, Jan, has made a name for himself in Franskraal, where he's opened the wonderful Strandveld Museum (see p85).

Oom At makes tea the old-fashioned way. He boils the kettle, throws some tea bags into a teapot and then plonks it on the hot stove so that it can brew *lekker* strong for a few minutes. There's an Emerald Dover Stove in the corner of the kitchen and lots of photos of his extended family. In most of the pictures there's either a wagon or somebody – usually *Oom* Attie – on horseback. Saddles and bridles are mounted on the wall close to the front door and with each one is an old leather

RIGHT: *Oom* Attie Fourie in one of the restored wagons he loves relaxing in (see p121).
FAR RIGHT: A rusty bike that's seen better days rests against a wall at the Napier Farm Stall.
OPPOSITE TOP: The quiet streets of Napier are typical of the small towns dotting the Overberg.
OPPOSITE MIDDLE: *Oom* Attie on one of his treks in memory of his forefathers, who traversed the country by ox wagon or donkey cart. The love of the open road courses through *Oom* Attie's veins, as his grandfather was a transporter who was accustomed to life on the move.
OPPOSITE BOTTOM LEFT: Pumpkins lined up on a garden wall sum up the essence of country life.
OPPOSITE BOTTOM RIGHT: Old farm implements and household goods find new life in a Napier store.

hat with a tie string. Berets aren't good when you're riding – you need something that you can tie *vas* so it doesn't blow away while you're galloping across the veld.

Attie grew up in Napier and spent lots of time with his grandfather who worked as a transporter and was used to loading up his wagon and trekking from one Overberg town to the next. Attie's education came from doing and watching rather than sitting behind a school desk and he likes to tell the story of how, when he had just started school, he went on a journey with his grandfather. The deal was that he should take his school reader with him and practise along the way but, as often happens, things didn't quite work out as planned.

As readers go, this was a particularly bad one involving a black cat and a baboon who were mates and spent time together. While the young Attie practised reading aloud, his grandfather's workers got more and more annoyed at just how unbelievable the story was. His grandfather got so irritated listening to them moaning that one night he grabbed the book and threw it away. Attie was on page five, and that's as far as he got with formal schooling. He subsequently taught himself to read and write.

Although his grandfather put an end to his school career, Attie went on to learn everything about working with his hands and handling animals. He's retired now but spends his time finding dilapidated old wagons, restoring them and using them on his famous treks. He's travelled from Namibia back to Napier with a span of donkeys. The journey took 85 days. Attie loves the old wagons so much that he's even restored one and put a bed in it. It's in the garden and the view over the hills and town is restorative. He prefers to sleep in the wagon rather than the house – especially on hot summer evenings when a man needs to feel the breeze on his face.

But Attie doesn't just journey with his wagons and donkeys. He's also keen on 'riding commando' across the countryside and he's ridden to the sea – a five-day journey away – more times than he cares to remember. But Attie doesn't go alone – he takes a group of children with him and it's not uncommon for him to ride while leading a pony and its really young rider. Or two. The kids love it, of course. Who wouldn't? You ride across farmland, sleep out in the open or camp in friendly farmers' barns. Supper is *boerewors* and *pap* around a fire, and in the early morning there are rusks and coffee that's brewed on the coals.

Attie believes it's good for children to spend time with horses. It keeps them out of trouble and they learn to take care of something. But now Attie is scaling down. He only has two riding horses, his donkeys to pull the *karretjies* and some chickens in a coop at the top of the field. The guinea fowl sleep with the chickens at night and Attie likes that.

We look at an old framed print of two lime-washed fishermen's cottages in a pretty bay. It looks like a romantic painter's idea of a quaint but unbelievable seaside village.

'That's Gansbaai back in the beginning,' says *Oom* At, pointing at the cottages. 'That was the boarding house and that was my granny's house. A pub is now on the site where the family house used to be.'

Pascal's

When singer Danièle Pascal and one of her best friends, Leonie Verster, bought a property in Napier, they each imagined a different life for themselves. Danièle thought it would be a good place to retire, while Leonie was looking for a place to escape for the weekends. Things didn't quite turn out as planned – at the beginning of 2003 they opened a restaurant, Pascal's, where Danièle would sing once in a while. It was going to be a weekends-only venue but the town has got so busy that this has all changed.

Why choose Napier? For Pascal it's because of the town's authenticity and beauty – and there's plenty of room for her vegetable garden – while for Leonie it's the 'ruralness' and 'farminess' of the area. For her, there's nothing nicer than sitting on her *stoep* and watching horses go by, or being woken by cocks crowing in the morning. Who could disagree?

DIE
KOSMAND
TEL 33
Coca-Cola

COUNTRY
JUNK
DESERVE
SHAKE
vote NNP
AFRICA
DESERVES
BETTER
YS KOUE
BIER
YS
2.00
Daar is
weer
hoop!

Ginger beer

Besides offering 'Warm, sexy bread,' the Moerse *Farm Stall also makes fantastic ginger beer. It's the perfect cooler on those sweltering summer days when the air is so still that even doing the simplest chores is too much effort. This is the time to lie under the olive tree near the reservoir and rickety windmill and get into the rhythm of swimming (mind the frogs at the edge) and knocking back litres of home brew.*

There's a ginger beer story that needs regular telling. It involves a group of plaasmeisies *sent off to boarding school during the 1940s. They longed for the tastes of home and, in order to recall those hot summer afternoons spent on their red polished verandahs overlooking the hills, they decided to make ginger beer based on their mothers' tried and tested recipes. They also added raisins to speed up the fermentation process because, well, they wanted that extra kick.*

Of course, brewing ginger beer wasn't on the school curriculum so the bottles were carefully stacked in their cupboards under the regulation puffy bloomers and industrial strength bras.

Later that week there was a volley of gunfire from the dormitory that sent the girls and teaches running to investigate. All but one of the bottles had shot its cork! The mess was legendary and apart from being grounded for 3 weeks, their underwear smelt like sweet ginger beer for days to come.

Moerse ginger beer

9 litres water
1.5 kg sugar
1 packet instant yeast
50 ml ginger
10 mg cream of tartare
Mint to decorate

Mix everything together until it has dissolved. Let it stand for 48 hours. Bottle and refrigerate. Serve ice-cold with lots of ice and a sprig of mint.

Bredasdorp

Established in 1838 by Michiel van Breda as a Dutch Reformed centre on Langefontein Farm, Bredasdorp is an important part of this dairy, wool and wheat farming region. Every town has to be famous for something and Bredasdorp gets the kudos for being the birthplace of merino sheep in South Africa. There's even a statue in honour of the woolly hero in the town. Of course, because it's the Overberg and nothing really happens here without a story, there's also a yarn behind how the merinos came about. Tragically it involves a suicide, an impoverished widow and a couple of shrewd businessmen.

While the *Kaapsche skape* in the early days of the Cape had enormous fat tails, they didn't have the wool that the settlers were looking for. When in the late 1780s Colonel Robert Jacob Gordon had the opportunity to take possession of imported merino rams and ewes from Spain, he didn't hesitate as he believed they had the characteristics he was looking for. Interestingly, it took five crossbreedings to produce the wool Gordon wanted – except he didn't live to see the results of his vision. He fell from grace and the Spanish demanded their sheep back. So he returned six sheep – keeping their offspring for himself. However Gordon's bad luck wasn't over and, when he was accused of treachery, he committed suicide. His impecunious widow was eventually forced to sell his flock. She sold three rams to a local farmer and the rest were shipped off to Australia where they formed the founding stock of the enormously successful Australian sheep industry. Back home in the Overberg, it didn't take long for the sheep to fall under the care of Michiel van Breda, who is heralded as the man who put sheep farming on the South African map.

What most visitors to the Overberg don't know – but these are the kinds of interesting facts you only ever find out over a cup of tea with a farmer's wife – is that the merino is the only sheep in the world that can produce as much as 10 to 15 percent of its own live mass in clean wool.

RIGHT: It takes an iron will to resist the treats at the *Moerse* Farm Stall in Napier. FAR RIGHT: Naghtwaght Farm is one of the oldest farms in Bredasdorp. OPPOSITE BOTTOM LEFT AND MIDDLE: There's no better way to start your day than with a slice of fresh bread made from the region's best grain. OPPOSITE TOP RIGHT: Bredasdorp was named after country baron Michiel van Breda. OPPOSITE BOTTOM RIGHT: The windmill at Soetevlei Farm, Bredasdorp, remains stationary for a change.

Bredasdorp's famous daughter

Author Audrey Blignaut is a daughter of the Overberg and has its sun and soil imprinted on her soul. She manages to capture this essence in her writing and has a loyal following who guard their copies of her books closely. Some of her best-loved titles are *Dit Reën Rose* (It Rains Roses) and *Die Rooi Granaat* (The Red Pomegranate). The titles say much about the area: which Overberg cottage doesn't have a jumble of beautiful roses in the garden and an unruly pomegranate tree in the backyard? And what child hasn't cracked open the fruit to get to the glistening jewels that lie embedded in the pithy white? Blignaut was born in 1916 and currently lives in Cape Town.

A shining light

When Ilse Appelgryn starting making candles at her home in Bredasdorp in 1994, she couldn't have foreseen just how well her little home industry would take off. Even the name she chose was modest – she called her company Kapula Candles, after her saying: 'I'm making a couple o' candles'. Over the decade, however, this 'couple' has grown to over 250 000 candles a month. The candles are made from top quality imported wax, wick and pigment and each is crafted and decorated by hand. Kapula Candles has also spread its light to the people of Bredasdorp. The company has a staff of over 200 permanent employees, all of whom are from the local community.

Elim

The wind plays havoc with the ladies' hats as they make their way up the road towards the church that dominates the village. This is definitely an occasion when three hands would be much better than two. One to hold down your full floral skirt and mischievous petticoat, the second to clutch your apricot pink hat and the third to guard your Bible and handbag. The men with their checked hats and black suits with white ties fare better. Two hands do it for them. One clasps a Bible, while the other stays free to shake hands with

TOP: An old-fashioned scale in an Elim shop brings back memories of a bygone era (see p125). ABOVE: The village's old water mill, built in 1828, is a National Monument. TOP RIGHT: Elim's peaceful main street hasn't changed significantly over the past few decades. Therein lies the village's charm – and its downfall (see text opposite). MIDDLE RIGHT: The Moravian Church is a sanctuary and forms the centre of village life. BOTTOM RIGHT: The entrance to the village of Elim – named after a Biblical oasis – is unpretentious but sincere.

friends and neighbours as they gather outside for a last quick smoke or a stand around in the sun. The women go in early, of course, and their voices swell and dip as they sing an impromptu hymn.

The inside of the church is beautiful in its all-white simplicity and expansive height. When the white curtains balloon inwards with the wind and the morning light falls on one of the congregants' high cheekbones, you'll wish you could paint like Vermeer to capture this moment of luminosity. And, when a lone voice rises above the hubbub to start the first hymn, you'll be hard-pressed not to cry silently and reach to ask your neighbour for one of the tissues she has tucked neatly under her watchstrap.

Elim is a strange village caught in a time warp that seems to have it perpetually looking over its shoulder to the 'good old days' when the mill worked and the gardens were bountiful. Its history as a Moravian mission station is well known. Soon after the Moravian Church took over the Hemel-en-Aarde leper colony (see p68), they bought a 7 500-hectare farm Vogelstruyskraal in the Strandveld with the intention of opening a mission station. In 1825 they called it Elim after the place where the Israelites rested once they'd made their hazardous journey through the Red Sea. The literal translation of Elim is 'palm tree arbour', but it also means 'sweet spring' – and the lyrical name goes some way to capture the village's picturesque charm. The names of the houses are equally welcoming – two of the best-kept cottages in the main street encourage passers-by to Hou Moed (Have Courage) and Kom Weer (Come Again). With their gardens bursting with ebullient dahlias, bright zinnias and abundant fig trees that drop big red gems of fruit, it's easy imagining doing both.

As often happens in small towns, everyone is somehow related – either through marriage or by blood and sometimes both – and the surnames you'll hear most often are Cloete, Engel and October. And, while most people leave the village to go to Cape Town to make money, some return earlier than they expected to because they miss the quality of life.

Emile Richter, not yet 40, was born in the village and grew up there before heading to town. After 15 years in the city, however, he's back to run the tourism information centre.

'The other day I was walking in the main road when I passed my neighbour's three-year-old in the street,' says Emile. 'She was on the way to the shop. Can you imagine that happening in the city? There you have to keep an eye on your children in case they come to harm. But in Elim you know that they are safe and either somebody will tell you, "Hey, I saw your child pass by here five minutes ago," or they'll pick her up and take her back home. You can't put a price on this sort of peace of mind.'

Apart from revelling in the pleasure of being home, Emile is also keen to stop the slow sense of decay that has crept through the village and stopped it from prospering. For the most part the old mission buildings are run-down – a pity because they're beautiful in a solid, functional way, with wide verandahs and big, inviting doors. You only have to look at the old sepia photos hanging in the water mill to get an idea of what a bustling place this used to be. The shop in the pictures is well stocked and there's an obvious feeling of abundance. The butchery is organised and there are plenty of photos of buxom, beaming women standing alongside the freshly-slaughtered carcasses of pigs and sheep. There are wagons of grain parked outside the mill waiting to be ground.

'We have so much to be proud of,' Emile explains, 'but people have stopped placing value on being resourceful and on being able to make things with their hands. When the Moravians came out from Germany and started the mission stations Genadendal and then Elim, they had to be able to do everything for themselves – from building their churches to growing their own food. They passed on these skills to the people who converted and to this day Elim still turns out some of the country's best thatchers. Unfortunately, though, people don't value this skill highly enough and I've seen too many men go to work for a pittance in the city for contractors who are happy to get rich off our backs. Elim thatchers should rather form a guild and work for themselves.'

And this is where the sense of nostalgia creeps in. In its heyday from the 1930s through to the early 1970s, Elim was busy and fruitful. Mr Ulrich Naumann worked as the Managing Director of the mission and was, indeed, a man on a mission. He introduced pig farming and his special recipe of Elim Cervelat Wurst became well known throughout the country and the bakery produced wonderful home-made bread with freshly-milled flour. Now the fields are neglected, the mill doesn't work and, if you stay in the town's only B&B, chances are you'll get store-bought bread for breakfast.

Emile, however, is keen to put Elim back on the map where it belongs. 'There's so much to treasure – the whole village is a National Monument and it's home to the only monument in the country commemorating the freeing of the slaves. The village is also famous for its everlastings and there are 102 species of fynbos that you won't find anywhere else. Elim heath or *Erica regia* is beautiful and the women still pick and pack the proteas and *sewejaartjies* that are exported overseas. My passion lies in letting other people know how unique Elim is. We've got our problems, make no mistake, but we've also got the biggest wooden water mill in the country, and the oldest working clock. This tells me that Elimers have a vision that goes way back – we just need that to become a reality again.'

Elim still turns out some of the country's best thatchers.

Blue cranes

Like the African black oystercatcher found along the Overstrand coastline, the blue crane (*Anthropoides paradisea*) is listed as critically endangered according to the IUCN Species Survival Commission's Red Data categories for threatened species. The numbers have decreased from about 100 000 in the early 1980s to about 20 000 birds at present.

This elegant, leggy bird with its floaty tail feathers is South Africa's national bird and graces our five cent coin, but this hasn't afforded the species the protection it needs to survive. The biggest threat to the birds are the farmers who poison them deliberately to stop them from trampling on their young crops. The other threat is posed by commercial tree plantations that destroy the birds' grassland breeding habitat.

Fortunately, Overbergers are increasingly proud of the 'Blues' and protection groups have been formed to try to educate farmers in crane-friendly practices. You can even go on blue crane guided tours.

Baardskeerdersbos

Wouldn't you love to have an address that lists Baardskeerdersbos as your home town? And when people ask you what it means you would say, 'Oh, it's a long story', and then you would have to stop a while and explain just two of the many possibilities. The most reasonable is that the town is named after the formidable spider that has fearsome-looking mandibles that would make any barber envious. As it turns out the mandibles are all for show and they're completely harmless. The spider is called the *baardskeerder* (the beard shaver), but is also known as the jerrymanglum. Now, that would also be a good name for town. 'Hi. My name is Pieter and I come from Jerrymanglum.'

The other option is far more romantic and has to do with an extremely hirsute farmer in desperate need of a good shave. So, when a travelling barber passed through the area, the man bequeathed his farm in exchange for spiffy short back and sides!

The name dates back to around the 1730s and the winds of change haven't blown through this village much since then, although the prospect of a tar road to link Gansbaai and Bredasdorp could change all this far too quickly. For the moment, however, there is a B'Bos store selling chips, coffee and the like. There's not much else except for a fanciful blue double-storey bus that's used as a holiday home – and some extremely eccentric characters that have become legends in their own lifetimes.

There's also the Baardskeedersbos *Orkes* (formally known as the Pavement Specials) that plays at local weddings, dances and festivals. Made up of people who have lived in the area for ages, the band plays a mixture of modern and traditional *boeremusiek* using instruments like the banjo, concertina and accordion. This is music that evolved around the camp fire and the songs are full of yearning and nostalgia. Their CDs have brilliant titles: *Strandveld Jolyt*, *Gooi Los* (mostly about fishermen and their passion for the sea, which is obvious considering most of the big fishing boats we saw had the same name), *Dêmmit Maar Dis Lekker* and *Kom Sing en Dans*.

OPPOSITE FAR LEFT, TOP AND BOTTOM: Images of this agricultural region. OPPOSITE TOP: The blue crane is South Africa's national bird. OPPOSITE BOTTOM RIGHT: Pincushion proteas are picked for export. THIS PAGE TOP: Protea picker on Heidehof Farm. ABOVE: *Oom* Snoekies is well known in Baardskeerdersbos – the entrance to his farm is designed to instil fear! LEFT: Protea nectar attracts a variety of birds. FAR LEFT: Leaving Elim behind for the distractions of the coast.

Wolvengat

Don't blink because you might miss it. That would be a pity because here's another choice town name and more of those gritty characters that populate the Overberg.

Just to give you a taste, there's a notice in Jenny's Handelhuis that reads:

Open most days about 10 or 11,
Occasionally as early as 8
But sometimes as late as 12 or 1
We close about 5.30 or 6,
Occasionally about 4 or 5
But sometimes as late as 10 or 11.

So, take it or leave it; like it or lump it, this is the way things are done in Wolvengat – with a sense of humour and an independent spirit. But, you can't get too shirty with Jenny and Gerard Bleeker who own the shop. They also own the only petrol pump and you can't afford to get caught with an empty tank and somebody disinclined to fill it.

At one point the dot on the map was known more formally as Viljoenshof and, in a weird bureaucratic mix up, it went from Wolvengat to Viljoenshof and now it's back to Wolvengat. How it happened goes something like this: the farm that eventually evolved into a sleepy settlement was originally called Wolvengat in honour of the brown hyenas or *strandwolwe* that still roam Pearly Beach and Buffeljagsbaai to this day. At the time, the hyenas had a lair (or *gat*) on the farm and the name made sense to people who – before a network of roads criss-crossed the country – navigated the wide-open spaces according to natural landmarks or hazards. (That's why you get Stormsvlei near Riviersonderend, for instance, because, if you're riding cross-country, best you know about the stormy marsh before you ride your trusty steed into it. Or there's Soetanysberg – Sweet Anise Mountain – where you can collect a fragrant herb that's good to use in cooking.)

But then the post office came to town. The post stamp they had said 'Viljoenshof' and, as officials thought Wolvengat sounded rude, they renamed the village Viljoenshof. All the old road signs in the area still direct you to this formal sounding town where you expect to find at least a church and a school. Today there's neither, although in the early 1900s there was a thriving school with 100 children. When the post office burnt down, residents decided they wanted the old name back, so now it's Wolvengat again.

For all the name changes, though, one thing remains the same: the fertile soil. And property prices have gone through the roof as more people arrive in search of a different way of life. There's talk that big dealers are buying up tracts of land for vineyards – and certainly when you take the gravel road back to the coast there are plenty of vines to be seen.

But, for now, it's hard to believe that much is happening. The local youths lie on the warm tarmac of the road that meanders through the town, waiting for the shop to open to get a hot pie and a cold Coke.

Spend time with Gerard and he'll fill you in on everything you need to know about the hamlet. He has a wonderful collection of memorabilia and many interesting stories about the good old days. But, while soaking up the tranquility and marvelling at the fynbos covering the hills, it's easy to believe that perhaps those good old days are here still. They're found in quiet spring mornings when there's thick dew on the fields, or in late autumn when the waning sun brushed on the treetops. Or when the owls call at night... .

RIGHT: Julian (left) and El-Jo Pieters (right), and Veronica Souls, enjoy a Saturday-afternoon donkey cart ride in Baardskeerdersbos. FAR RIGHT: Elim has attracted all kinds of artists and craftspeople keen to express themselves and gain inspiration from the country way of life. OPPOSITE TOP LEFT: Langrug Cottage at Soetevlei Farm. OPPOSITE MIDDLE LEFT: Red hot pokers make a stand against the blue sky. OPPOSITE TOP RIGHT AND MIDDLE RIGHT: Soetevlei is the second largest fresh water vlei in the southern hemisphere. OPPOSITE BOTTOM: Gerard Bleeker behind the counter at Jenny's Handelshuis, Wolvengat. He's an avid collector of memorabilia and old stories. Make sure you stop by and get him to tell you a few.

'I could never dare say, but I have always thought, that I do not want to go to heaven. I would just like to stay here in our house, in our village. It is the prettiest place in the whole world.' – Audrey Blignaut

Favourites

You can't leave the area without ...

- Admiring the old wood-burning stoves at the Dassiesfontein farmstall on the N2. Imagine how nice one would look in the corner of your kitchen and how comforting it would be to sit around it on a wet winter's evening.
- Buying a strand of plaited onions. After all, Caledon Globes are famous for their sweet nuttiness. Now's the perfect time to make a caramelised onion tart.
- Lounging around in the Caledon hot springs (see p115).
- Pulling over to watch a pair of blue cranes doing their striking courtship dance (see p129).
- Attending Napier's *soetpatat* fees. If potatoes don't do it for you, make sure you're around for the local horse show. Riders and carters come from miles around to show off their horses and their equestrian skills.
- Tucking into a fresh *vetkoek* from the *Moerse* Farm Stall in Napier (see p124).
- Feeling a little melancholic while listening to Danièle Pascal performing her famous repertoire of Edith Piaf and Jacques Brel numbers at Pascal's in Napier while you tuck into bouillabaisse or a hearty lamb shank (see p122).
- Admiring the fields of yellow canola that turn the landscape into a painter's dream.
- Riding 'on commando' with Oom Attie. Easter weekend usually sees a big ride that people book for well in advance (see p121).
- Visiting the wonderful Shipwreck Museum in Bredasdorp. They have a fantastic collection of furniture that has come off ships that ran into trouble on the treacherous coast and you'll get a sense of what life at sea was like.
- Attending a church service in Elim after spending the night in the village's only B&B (see p125).
- Visiting Geelkop Nature Reserve. Ask your guide to point out which species of protea is endemic to this area. The reserve is owned by the Moravian Church and home to the rare Elim dwarf fynbos, *Protea pudens*. There's also an easy seven-kilometre hike you can do, as well as a circular drive with panoramic views.

OPPOSITE CLOCKWISE FROM TOP: Soetevlei Farm, Bredasdorp; Traditional skills, such as shoemaking, are still practised in villages like Napier; Wheatfields, Caledon; Bredasdorp's famous merinos; Rose's Art and Toy World, Napier (see p121); Detail on the Moravian Church, Elim.

RIGHT TOP TO BOTTOM: Elim's quaint cottages – the whole village is a National Monument; Golden wheatfields are a familiar sight in the Caledon area; Country towns like Caledon, Bredasdorp and Napier are working agricultural towns where the farming co-op has pride of place in the main street, and it's not uncommon to find tractors parked in the streets alongside *bakkies* laden with produce; The famous Napier Farm Stall and Restaurant (see p120).

ABOVE: The dark blue mountains near Caledon form a dramatic backdrop to the area's farms. RIGHT AND FAR RIGHT: Pomegranates and globe onions are products of the Overberg soil and would make the perfect still life for a budding Vermeer. OPPOSITE TOP: Stacks of thatching grass, Soetevlei Farm, Elim. The village still produces some of South Africa's best thatchers (see p127). OPPOSITE MIDDLE: Bredasdorp is also known for its goose down products, which are sold at Bel Don (see opposite).

Contact numbers

Bredasdorp Tourism: 028-424-2584
Caledon Tourism: 028-212-1511
Elim Tourism and Heritage Centre: 028-482-1806
Napier Tourism: 028-423-3325

Bel Don (Bredasdorp): 028-425-1166
Bredasdorp Shipwreck Museum: 028-424-1240
Geelkop Private Nature Reserve (Elim): 028-482-1806
Grootberg Hiking Trail (Napier): 028-423-3325
Heuningberg Nature Reserve: (Bredasdorp): 028-424-2584
Jenny's Handelshuis (Wolvengat): 028-482-1985
Kapula Candles (Bredasdorp): 028-424-2829
Moerse Farm Stall (Napier): 028-423-3334
Napier All Sorts: 028-423-3861
Napier Farm Stall: 028-423-3440
Overberg Crane Group: 028-214 8905 or 082-676-1734
Pascal's (Napier): 028-423-3146
Rose's Art and Toy World (Napier): 028-423-3894
Voorhoede 4x4 Route (Caledon): 083-273-8356

Where to stay

www.overberginfo.com
Caledon Spa and Casino: 028-214-5100
Earl of Clarendon (Bredasdorp): 028-425-1420
Elim Guest House: 028-482-1806.
Luton Lodge (Napier): 028-423-3440
Overberg Guest House (Bredasdorp): 028-425-3223
Sunbird Fynbos Reserve B&B (Napier): 028-423-3049

Valley of the Indigo Mountains

GREYTON and GENADENDAL

THE COURT YARD
Aartworks Gallery
Mola
von Geusau Chocolates
von Geusau Chocola
Café Herbert

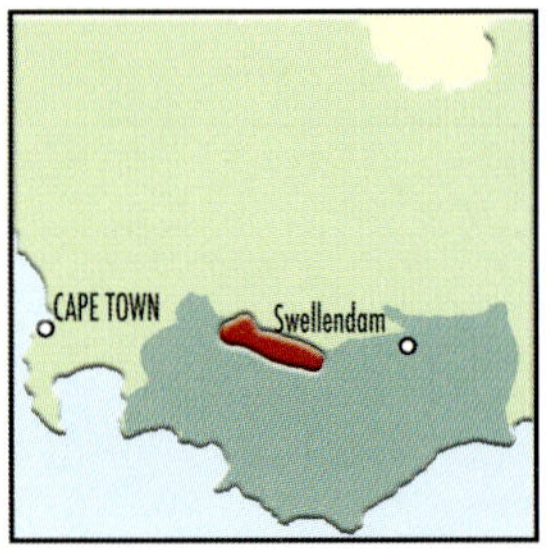

Spend time in places like Greyton and Genadendal and before you know it you'll be doing the strangest things, like buying a pumpkin the size of a large child because it looks so beautiful and you're convinced you'll make pumpkin fritters like the ones you remember eating when you were growing up. That's the thing with these sorts of villages: they're beautiful, charming and completely intoxicating.

The grace of Greyton

Way back in the middle of the eighteenth century the Dutch East India Company established a company cattle farm in the area called Zoete Melks Valleij (Sweet Milk Valley), no doubt because the area at the foot of the towering Zondereind Mountains was so fertile and there was plenty of water for abundant crops and healthy livestock. At the time, the farm was managed by Baas Theunissen. His son, Marthinus Theunissen Jnr. went on to obtain the farm Weltevreden (Greyton) which was situated between Zoete Melks Valleij and Baviaans Kloof (Genadendal), as well as many other farms. Theunissen was obviously an exceptionally wealthy landowner at the time because he also owned the beautiful Vergelegen in Somerset West. Weltevreden was later sold to another wealthy landowner and old Cape personality, Hendrik Cloete, who also owned Groot Constantia.

When the Cape became a permanent possession of the British Crown in 1815, the 'English invasion' of the Overberg began. Herbert Vigne, son of a London merchant and descendant of a Huguenot who had fled to England, purchased the farm Weltevreden in 1846. Herbert was related by marriage to both Lady Anne Barnard and Sir George Grey, Governor of the Cape. In 1854 he subdivided his farm into 120 plots and called the new village Greyton, after Sir George Grey. Grey is said to have assisted in the design of the village. The sale of the plots was advertised in the news sheets of the day and purchasers from all over the Cape bought land at prices ranging from five to eleven pounds sterling a plot.'
(Extract taken from Greyton: Your Guide to the Beauty and Enchantment of this Unique Environment' – Greyton Tourism.)

McGregor, immediately over the Sonderend Mountains, was established soon after Greyton. Only then it was called Lady Grey in honour of Sir Grey's wife. Herbert Vigne was responsible for building the footpath between the villages and some of the older residents remember walking to McGregor to play a game of tennis, and then walking back home again.

One of the attractions of Greyton is the town's pretty Victorian architecture and many of the holiday homes and stores have been lovingly restored.

Two buildings have been declared National Monuments: the Post House and the building occupied by Ploom's Pottery. The Post House dates back to 1860 when it housed Greyton's first post office. The building was made the old-fashioned way, with rock foundations and mud-and-straw bricks

Getting mail in those days was a significantly slower process than it is today. Mr Outa Karools made the long journey to Caledon three times a week by horse and cart to fetch the post. In the evening, he used to announce his arrival to the residents by blowing on his horn.

Today, the Post House is a popular upmarket guesthouse that oozes country charm and hospitality.

Changes in town

Up until the mid-1970s Greyton was a sleepy paradise untouched by apartheid where black and white families farmed side by side as they had done for generations. After 1976, however, the town changed dramatically when coloured families who had lived there for generations were moved to a new 'township' known as Heuwelkroon. The vacated houses were snapped up by people looking for weekend retreats and the gentrification of the village began. Not surprisingly, there are currently several land claims laid against properties in Greyton.

Paradise is not without its flaws and today there's a quiet war being fought for the soul of this rural community. You can tell a lot about a place by reading the local newspaper. *The Greyton Sentinel* is bristling with news and opinions that hint at the issues. Towards the end of his outgoing editorial in April 2004, the impassioned editor, Alan Blain, wrote:

There was a time not long ago when all races lived side by side in Greyton. No more! There was a time when many farming families, [who were] largely Afrikaans speaking, predominated in Greyton. No more. There was a time when everyone in Greyton knew each other and life was uncomplicated and easy. No more. Each new season has

PREVIOUS SPREAD: Mountains in the Greyton area and other scenes from the region. THIS PAGE, TOP: Autumn trees line a quiet street in Greyton. LEFT: Greyton has a number of excellent restaurants, such as the Oak & Vigne, where you can linger under shady trees with a coffee and your newspaper. ABOVE: Everyone wants a cottage in the country as picturesque as this one near the Greyton Nature Reserve (see p142).
OVERLEAF LEFT: Winter avenue – there are plenty of secluded lanes to disappear down and each season they take on a different character. RIGHT: A familiar country scene on the dusty country road between Greyton and Riviersonderend, with the beautiful Sonderend Mountains in the distance (see p145).

its own challenges. The challenge of the new season about to take hold in Greyton is no less than a challenge for the very soul of this village and its unique lifestyle.

Brave hearts, fearless protagonists of rural values, and dedicated soldiers for the status quo will be needed to ensure Greyton does not bend to the enormous pressure and seductive allure of money and avarice. For then it will finally and for always lose the vital ingredient that makes all the natural beauty worth enjoying. Conversely without that ingredient all the beauty and splendour of the scenery will be as shallow as a 50c postcard. That ingredient is its wonderful humanity.

There's more in the paper that describes fears that Greyton might end up overdeveloped, and mention of how a golf course was proposed and vetoed – for now. This is small-town stuff that isn't peculiar to this pretty little village – it does describe the potential fate of many small towns which, once they're discovered, end up losing the very charm that made them so glorious in the first place.

Many towns in the Overberg are faced with a similar dilemma but it's just that in Greyton the stakes seem particularly high. The quaint village is astonishingly pretty, and the amount of wealth that has poured into it astronomical. On high days and holidays the streets are lined with huge 4x4s and the town's residents are increasingly sophisticated. That's not a bad thing in itself, but it's not so good when property prices rise to such an extent that the people who work and service the village can no longer afford to live there. To give you some measure of how prices have escalated, five years ago a house that cost 350 000 rand could now be sold for 1.8-million rand.

Aside from the editorial, there are advertisements in *The Sentinel* that also sum up the metamorphosis the village has undergone in the past few decades. The first is for a lifestyle store called Violet Dream and yet another for Victorian bathrooms. Now, individually they don't mean that much, but collectively they do speak of a time quite different from an era when advertisements rather offered cheap kraal manure and reliable tractor repairs.

It's clear that the agrarian nature of the village has, for the most part, vanished forever. Now people are more interested in eating well and acquiring fashionable décor for their holiday homes, than in growing a good summer crop that will be enough to feed their family of eight children and four grandparents.

Tale of a Greyton 'tannie'

Anna Richter is from the old Greyton. Her house has escaped any making over: there's no trace of reproduction *broekie* lace and absolutely no factory-made 'distressed' country-style furniture. Anna was born on a farm outside Greyton and as a child came to live with her grandparents in the house where she still lives today. All the children in her family moved to live with *ouma* and *oupa* so they could go to school. At one point there were eight children in the small house and, although Anna can't figure out where they all slept, she remembers growing up happy and carefree.

It's late summer and Anna's garden is overgrown and the weeds out the back are flourishing. There's a hand-held plough lying next to the sweet potatoes but it looks unused.

'When I was younger and stronger,' she says impatiently, 'there weren't any weeds here. Our garden was a paradise where we grew all we needed. We had *naartjies*, avocados, pears, pomegranates, oranges, lemons, sweet potatoes and beans. I miss the days when white families lived next door to black families. If somebody needed help ploughing, you would just shout and they would come, and we would do the

Greyt lemon syrup

Kay Cuttler is well known for her lemon syrup, which she sells at the local Saturday morning market as well as to customers in Cape Town. It's perfect for those sweltering Overberg summer days when it's too hot to do anything except alternate between lying in a cold bath and collapsing on your stoep *under the* rietdak*. On days like these, it's even too hot to read and you can only start moving again when the sun starts dipping behind the mountains after seven in the evening. A tall frosty glass of lemon juice with plenty of ice and soda water is just what you need to perk you up.*

Kay's not entirely sure how she became the Lemon Juice Lady. As a former personnel manager she didn't have plans to retire to Greyton to spend lots of hours grating lemon zest and squeezing lemons. But that's what she's doing – and loving every minute of it. It all came about when her neighbour gave Kay a small bag of lemons four years ago. When Kay asked her what she should do with them, the friend also gave her an old Christmas card with a recipe for lemon syrup scribbled on the back and suggested Kay give it a bash. She did and now she's churning out her sweet, tangy juice for Greyton residents and visitors. Kay is most fortunate to be supplied with organic lemons from Bram and Davida Wind from the village, and visitors can, for a small charge, call in to their orchard in Vigne Street and pick their own lemons. Even if you don't live in the country, at least for a morning you can pretend you're the real McCoy.

Here's Kay's old-fashioned recipe – just like granny used to make it:

Grate rind from enough lemons to fill two cups. Squeeze sufficient lemons to make 1½ litres of lemon juice. (Kay has burnt out two electric juicers in quick succession!)

Add 4 kg sugar (or less) followed by
50 g Epsom salt
50 g tartaric acid
100 g citric acid and pour 3.4 litres of boiling water over the mixture.
Stir well until all the sugar has dissolved
Stand overnight for about 8 hours. Remember to cover the mixture with a clean cloth.
Strain and bottle in screw top bottles.
Makes approximately 9 x 350 ml bottles.

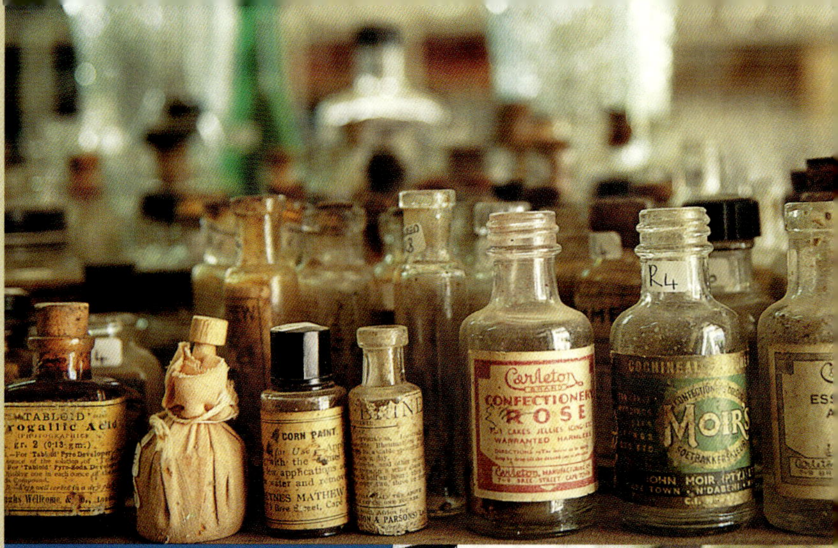

TOP RIGHT: Bric-à-brac fills Greyton's quaint shops. CENTRE LEFT: The historic Post House (see p138). CENTRE RIGHT: Don't leave without visiting Von Geusau's chocolate shop. RIGHT: Poppies enliven one of Greyton's abundant gardens. FAR RIGHT AND OPPOSITE: When you're relaxing at Greyton Lodge – built as a trading store in 1882 – it's easy to forget that the city's just over an hour's drive away.

same for them. Or I would sew dresses for their girls in exchange for their labour. In those days people used to start working when it was still dark. Now, if you do get help in the garden, nobody will start doing anything before eight in the morning. A lot else has changed. In those days we didn't have to spray, but now you've got to spray for everything if you want any fruit.'

Anna can tell you how Greyton has changed since the English arrived over 20 years ago and the gentrification of the town began. Back when everyone ploughed with an ox or donkey, there were over 800 members in the Dutch Reformed Church alone and people travelled in from the surrounding farms to attend the service each Sunday. There were donkey carts and horses in every field and you got up with the chickens and went to bed soon after dark.

For all the changes, though, remnants of small village life remain. Ask for directions and nobody will give you a street name; they will rather tell you to look out for the low wall and a front garden full of roses or 'the big oak tree with a swing for my grandchildren'.

And, because there is no chemist in Greyton, when anyone goes through to Caledon – about an hour's drive away – they know to drop in at the chemist there to see if anyone from the village needs their medicine collected. Back home in Greyton, they drop it off at Zippy's, the local supermarket, where everyone picks up their deliveries.

Greyton Nature Reserve

The Greyton Nature Reserve lies on the steep southern slopes of the Sonderend Mountains, which form part of the Cape Folded Belt. At 2 200 hectares it is the third largest reserve in the Western Cape and is a botanist's paradise. At least 22 indigenous trees can be found here – mostly in ravines where they're protected from fires that sweep across the mountainside. The trees include mountain cedar, wild almond, rooiels and keurboom. Some with more unusual names are the *taaibos*, silky bark bastard saffron, spoonwood and forest monkey plum.

When it comes to flowers, you'll be treated to watsonias, chincherinchees, aloes, disas and ground orchids. There's also a pelargonium that is unique to Greyton called the *Pelargonium greytonense*. And, when you're not admiring the views or looking out for birds, keep your eyes peeled for spoor – there are lots of small animals on these mountains, including grysbok, klipspringer, rhebok, blackfooted cat – and plenty of snakes.

There are a variety of walks in the reserve. You might want to tick off the Haardepeerkloof (Hard Pear Ravine) and Gifkloof (Poison Ravine) walks. If these aren't enough, there's also the Maermanskloof (Thin Man's Ravine) walk. Although it's obvious that most are named after the trees in the area, nobody's sure how Maermanskloof got its name. Perhaps a particularly thin man first marked out the route, or that's how you feel when you've been hiking for a couple of hours!

For all the changes, remnants of small village life remain.

The 'leiwater' system

There's something romantic about a village that is governed by a *leiwater* system. The *slote* bubble and rush with clear, cold water and on a hot summer's afternoon you're bound to feel nothing but pure joy as you pull up the little wooden or metal sluice that allows the refreshing coolness to rush into your furrows and through your garden. The *leiwater* speaks of a different era when people kept fit, not by going to the gym, but rather by digging in their vegetable gardens and developing good biceps by lifting sacks of grain to be milled into bread.

This, then, is Greyton. The streets are lined with ancient oak trees and nearly every garden has an unruly quince hedge, a gnarled fig tree and a pomegranate tree – watered, of course, by *leiwater* that starts at the top of the village and makes its way through the hamlet purely with the help of gravity.

Like any good Huguenot, Herbert Vigne was a Francophile and, after a visit to France, came back inspired by the extensive canal system he saw there. So, when the original farm was divided into plots, they were laid out with two things in mind – each family needed enough land to be self sufficient and each erf had to have access to water. After all, there was no point in planting vegetables if you couldn't water them! An erf that had access to the *lei* was known as a 'wet' erf. No access to the *lei* and your plot was a 'dry' erf.

While Greyton may no longer be inhabited by a hardy breed of vegetable gardeners, *leiwater* still plays an important role in village life. There's a Water Bailiff, a *Leiwater* Committee and regular meetings to monitor just what's going on. Residents still plan their social lives around when it's their turn for the water to come through and a few friendships have been broken over stolen water and sluice gates that mysteriously jam open in the night. There is also the occasional three a.m. phone call to one or another water monitor to complain anxiously about the mysterious non-arrival of someone's allocated water. When this happens, men pull on coats over their pyjamas, grab their torches and walk up the line to find the offending party. Since this is a small town, everyone knows the identity of the usual suspects and they're generally not difficult to find.

There are other things worth knowing about *leiwater*. Sometimes estate agents 'forget' to tell city-bred buyers (who don't know to ask) whether the erf they're fantasising about is wet or not, and this has lead to the occasional hefty dispute. Even more infuriating for residents are absentee homeowners who arrive at the weekend to find their gardens wilting and automatically open their sluice gates – not thinking about the people ten houses down who have been waiting all week for their allocation. Interesting stuff – and the very thing that gives small town living its texture and character.

The Sonderend Mountains

These towering peaks form an imposing backdrop to Greyton and Genadendal, as well as an impenetrable barrier separating them from the interior. McGregor, for instance, is just over the mountains – but getting there by road means a long detour. You could, of course, get there by foot via the Boesmanskloof Traverse, the only gap in the mountains. The 17-kilometre hike is stunning – with wonderful views, steep gorges and scenic waterfalls. Most people choose to do the walk over two days, spending a night in McGregor, but it can be done in a day if you're really fit. The Riviersonderend Nature Reserve stretches over this range and provides a protected haven for flora and fauna.

OPPOSITE LEFT: The *leiwater* system in Greyton and Genadendal is carefully regulated. OPPOSITE RIGHT: Greyton is a gardener's paradise. ABOVE: The Sonderend Mountains. LEFT: A graceful heron takes to the air. OVERLEAF LEFT: Farm worker, Swartrivier Farm, Greyton. OVERLEAF TOP: A candelabra flower, also known as *tolbos*. OVERLEAF MIDDLE: Genadendal's quaint post office. OVERLEAF BOTTOM: Genadendal's homes show unique touches, such as this door decorated with a cross made of flowers.

Genadendal

Genadendal feels like an odd mixture of things. How can you not fall in love with the donkeys that loiter near the beautiful Moravian church, the shutters with a heart motif cut out of them, the old mill and the rickety turnstile that takes you to the famous pear tree and old cemetery? There's also the smell of warm cut grass, the bright rows of marigolds and thatching grass laid out to dry. Everything about these details is lovely.

But, before you get to the old mission station, you turn into a village that seems strangled by poverty. How else could you explain the groups of men sitting around during the working week, or the young girls with curlers in their hair and babies on their hips? Unlike Greyton, Genadendal – the oldest mission station in the country – has escaped all gentrification.

Many of the village cottages are dilapidated and neglected, or patched with odd bits and pieces of corrugated iron. In its heyday at the beginning of the 1800s, craftsmen from the village were world-renowned for the knives they produced, and the narrow streets were busy with coppersmiths, hatters, cobblers, masons, blacksmiths, tanners, carpenters and wagon-wrights. It is tragic that a mission station that used to pride itself on self-sufficiency and craftsmanship is sinking down due to socio-economic and socio-political reasons.

History of the village

Genadendal, which means Valley of Grace, was originally called Baviaanskloof (Baboon Ravine) and was established in 1738 by the young Moravian missionary, Georg Schmidt. He arrived at a time when the Khoekhoen – already suffering under the influx of white farmers – were reeling from a smallpox epidemic to which they had no immunity. As a people they were on the verge of extinction and, against enormous odds, Schmidt formed a small congregation and taught the Khoekhoen to read and write. His good works came unstuck, however, when he began baptising the converts and the Dutch clergy based in Cape Town threw up their hands in horror. According to them, Schmidt was not an ordained minister and therefore had no right to administer the sacraments. In 1743 Schmidt was forced to return to Europe a disappointed man.

The mission station was abandoned until almost 50 years later when three missionaries returned to resume Schmidt's work. A famous story from Genadendal is that, when the men returned to the forsaken mission station, they met up with an old woman, Magdalena, who still had the Bible she had been given decades before when she had been baptised by Schmidt. Although nearly blind, Magdalena had treasured her Bible safely wrapped in a skin until the missionaries returned to their flock at Genadendal. Her Bible takes pride of place in the village's Cultural History Museum (see p151).

The three missionaries, like their predecessor Schmidt, also faced a frosty welcome by the Dutch Church at the Cape. Once again there were all sorts of objections to the work the missionaries were doing and they were initially prohibited

from building a chapel or church and they had to meet in the open or in their rudimentary cottages. They were even refused permission to ring a bell to call the children to school and the congregation to assemble. British occupation changed this, however, and by 1800 the first church was completed, but it soon became too small for the rapidly expanding congregation.

The Khoekhoen laws of 1808 instituted by the colonial government only served to boost the mission station – although this couldn't have been further from their intention. Under these laws, all Khoekhoen without a fixed abode were liable to be forced into farm labour. Given the dire conditions on farms, the mission stations – which provided access to land in return for conversion to Christianity – quickly became attractive alternatives and it's hardly surprising that formerly nomadic people streamed into the mission stations. Genadendal was so successful that at one point it was the largest settlement in the Colony after Cape Town.

But, it wasn't just the church authorities that were unhappy. A group of Strandveld farmers also threatened to put an end to the missionary work. It's not hard to understand why. At the time, the farmers were largely illiterate and were enormously unhappy about the idea of an educated and skilled underclass. They also faced an economic crisis, because of potential labourers that flocked to Genadendal instead.

But, despite all the political machinations, Genadendal flourished until the end of the nineteenth century and, significantly, the first Teachers' Training College in South Africa was built there in 1838. Genadendal also opened the first guest house and chemist shop in the interior and in 1830 it had one of the best public lending libraries at the Cape.

Things began to unravel in the 1860s, however, when factories began producing mass products that were much cheaper and people turned away from the hand-crafted items Genadendal was famous for. Residents had to leave the village and head to the city in search of work, which brought with it all kinds of social problems.

Legislation at the time was also far from equitable and the Communal Reserve Act of 1909 for Mission Stations, which granted inhabitants occupational rights only but prevented

TOP: Activities in Genadendal still centre around the church square. MIDDLE: Khoekhoen-style pottery made by locals. ABOVE AND RIGHT: The Pear Tree and Moravian Church are two historic sights. FAR RIGHT: Detail of one of the charming houses. OPPOSITE TOP: The Genadendal Information Centre is also a crafts centre. OPPOSITE BOTTOM LEFT AND RIGHT: Fresh bread is available from the bakery, and garden produce is turned into preserves.

Eugenia berry jelly

There's something enormously satisfying about making things from your garden, as any industrious Greytonian will tell you. A couple of years ago Ann Shone noticed that, come autumn, the dogs and cows in the village enjoyed eating the bright red berries from the Eugenia hedges and so, having been a Home Economics teacher for many years, she came up with the recipe for berry jelly. It's got a delicate flavour and is good served with meat or cheese.

2 kg berries (pick when just ripe)
2 large lemons
4 large apples

Wash the berries and place them in a large pot, just covering with water. Slice lemons finely, pips, core and all. Slice apples including skin and core. Add lemons and apples to berries and bring mixture to the boil, then simmer for about 1 hour until reduced and pulped. Strain everything through a muslin or similar cloth overnight.

When the dripping has stopped, measure the quantity of liquid. For each 1 litre of juice, add 750 g sugar. Boil juice and sugar together, only stirring until the sugar has dissolved. When the mixture forms a skin when placed on a cold saucer, or drips from a wooden spoon in large drops, remove any scum and cool slightly. Finally, pour into sterilised hot jars and seal.

Cooking with quinces

Everyone in Greyton has a quince tree or hedge, but quinces are awkward fruit. They look delicious and produce pretty flowers but they're strange to eat. They're hard and tart and have a peculiar grainy texture. Although quinces are certainly making a comeback and are starting to appear in overseas foodie magazines, they do need all the help they can get and are best eaten cooked. Some people love stewed quince with ice cream, while others believe it's the perfect ingredient to add to apple pie, because the uncompromising quince gives an interesting hint of woodiness among the sweetness of the apples.

Here's an old recipe for quince cheese. You serve it with cold meats, as the fruit's tartness works well with the richness of meat. Once set, the cheese is firm enough to be turned out on a plate and thinly sliced.

Quince cheese

Wash fruit and remove blemishes.
Chop (peel and all) and place in pan, covering with water and cook until mixture has reduced and is soft and pulpy.
Cool slightly, then press pulp through nylon-type sieve.
Measure pulp and add sugar as follows:
For every 500 g of pulp add 400 g of sugar.
Cook pulp and sugar together, dissolving the sugar, and then for a further 30 minutes, stirring occasionally until thick and there is no free liquid visible.
Place in wide-necked containers and seal with wax and airtight lids.

ABOVE: Genadendal's old water mill has been lovingly restored and is still used to grind meal. RIGHT: There are remnants of a bygone lifestyle wherever you look. RIGHT TOP AND BOTTOM: The shelves of the Oak and Vigne in Greyton groan with local produce, and a visitor enjoys a quiet moment on a window seat. OPPOSITE: The Sonderend Mountains (see p145).

them from getting property rights, caused an enormous rift between the missionaries and residents. The final blow came in 1926 when the Teachers' Training College was closed down by the Department of Public Education who argued that coloured people didn't need tertiary education if they were going to be employed on local farms.

Dr Isaac Balie is a committed Christian who can trace his family history six generations back to the Khoekhoen people of Genadendal. He works as local historian and Director of the Mission Museum.

'Today Genadendal, with its 3 500 registered occupants, is a forgotten, remote, underdeveloped and degraded village,' he explains. 'Not even the new democratic dispensation or the former State President, Mr Mandela, in renaming his official residence Genadendal, in 1995, could change its plight. Many residents pray now for spiritual revival that will save the community from total destruction. They stand firm on the Biblical promise, according to the sermon on the Mount: "But seek ye first the kingdom and His righteousness, and all these things shall be added unto you" (Mat. 6:33).'

There's always the chance for redemption and rebirth and hopefully Genadendal will soon experience another 'golden age'. For starters, each year the museum reaps honeybush tea from plants nearby and packages this fragrant tea for sale at the museum shop. They also make honeybush iced tea – the perfect thirst quencher on a blistering hot summer's day. It's a small start, but there are plenty of Biblical stories of humble beginnings and grand finales.

Cultural History Museum

The Cultural History Museum makes for a fascinating visit. The actual museum is housed in the building that was the first teachers' training college that opened in 1838. There are 15 exhibition rooms containing different things – household goods, musical instruments, a wonderful collection of old family portraits, printing presses and medical equipment. But the museum doesn't stand alone. It's part of a collection of buildings clustered around the church square. The Moravian Church – like all mission churches – is beautiful in its simplicity. The buildings include the old water mill, which has been restored, and the wonderful nursery and garden. There's also the Information Centre that doubles as a bakery and arts and crafts centre. Be prepared for the unexpected glimpses you might happen upon: somebody praying quietly in the church, piles of sweet-smelling thatch lined up against a thick white wall waiting to be used, or the smell of freshly baked bread.

Favourites

You can't leave the area without ...

- Spending a morning wandering around Greyton. You can also hire a bicycle from the local tourism office if you're keen to cover more ground. Be sure to go down as many side streets as possible – it's where the treasures of old Greyton lie.
- Sleeping over at the Post House. Choose a room named after your favourite Beatrix Potter character and make yourself at home together with the hotel cats. Luckily, the hotel has recently undergone a transformation and is not nearly as twee as the historic room names suggest. The hotel now has some funky new chefs, a hip front-of-house team and cool music in the bar and restaurant.
- Doing what the café society does and have coffee or lunch at the Oak & Vigne with your newspaper and dog for company.
- Waiting patiently for Daisy the cow to move out of the road in her good time. No hooting allowed.
- Going to the Greyton Saturday morning market.
- Getting energetic and doing the hike from Greyton to McGregor. You can stay over at Whipstock Farm for the night before heading back to Greyton the following day.
- Playing tennis on the old courts in the middle of the village. Be sure to look at some of the old photos of gentlewomen playing a game in their long dresses and hats.
- Hunting the elusive black bass in the beautiful Sonderend River during summer.
- Roaming around the historic part of Genadendal. The museum is fascinating and, if you time your visit right, you will be able to buy freshly baked bread made with flour ground at the local water mill.
- Hiking the Genadendal Hiking Trail. This 28-kilometre hike will take you through rugged mountains and cool kloofs. You can also swim at Groot and Klein Koffiegat (Big and Little Coffee Pools) – evocative names for pretty pools on the route.

TOP: Relaxing in the bar at the Post House in Greyton is a long-standing tradition. ABOVE: The donkeys in Genadendal have the run of the town and doze in the church square on hot summer's days. RIGHT: Genadendal's gardens are just as pretty as Greyton's. FAR RIGHT: Jan Bloed with his ox wagon, Greyton. OPPOSITE TOP LEFT: The area around Greyton and Genadendal is a botanist's paradise. TOP RIGHT: Swartrivier Farm, Greyton. BOTTOM LEFT: Interior of the Moravian Church, Genadendal. BOTTOM RIGHT: The Post House in Greyton has recently been renovated and the bathroom in the honeymoon suite is an interesting mixture of old and new.

ABOVE: Overview of Greyton.
RIGHT TO FAR RIGHT: Many village homes are National Monuments; an old car – evidence of a different way of life; a clock in the historic mission printing room in Genadendal; 'Jesus Makes the Difference' – the door of a house in Genadendal; a quaint village *stoep*.
ABOVE: Golden fields of wheat line the roads near Caledon.

Contact numbers

Genadendal Information: 028-251-8582 or 251-8291
Greyton Tourism: 028-254-9414

Genadendal Cultural History Museum: 028-251-8582
Genadendal Hiking Trail: 028-425-5020
Greyton–McGregor Hiking Trail – Boesmanskloof Hike: 028-254-9414
Greyton Mountain Bike Trail: 028-254-9414
Greyton Nature Reserve: 028-254-9414
Greyton Riding Centre: 028-254-9009
The Oak & Vigne Café (Greyton): 028-254-9037
Von Geusau Chocolates (Greyton): 028-254-9100
Zippy's (Greyton): 028-254-9712

Where to stay

www.overberginfo.com
Acorns on Oak (Greyton): 028-254-9567
Blue Crane Guest House (Greyton): 028-254-9839
Greyton Lodge: 028-254-9876
Potato Patch (Greyton): 082-411-7671
The Post House (Greyton): 028-254-9995

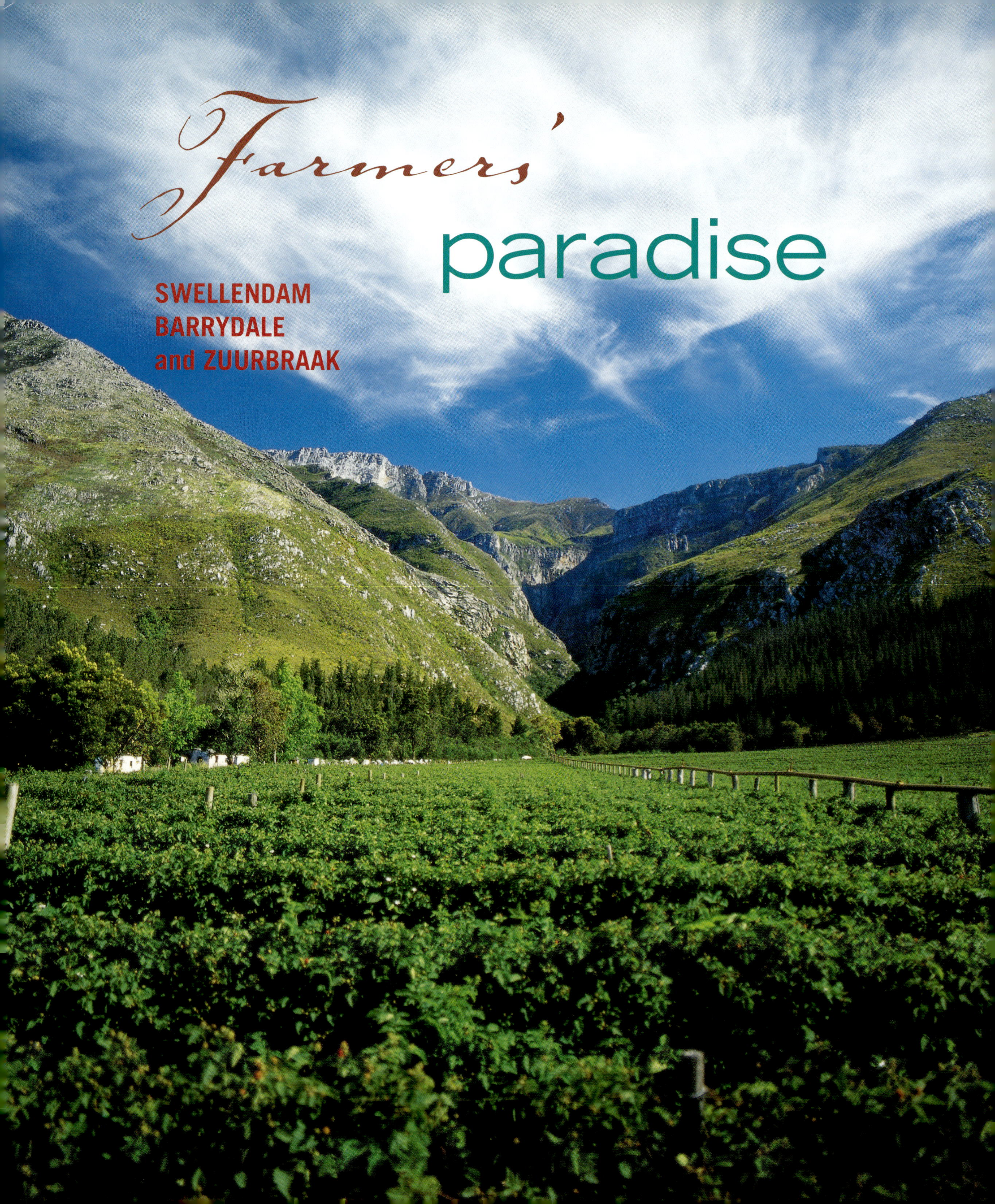
Farmers'
paradise
SWELLENDAM
BARRYDALE
and ZUURBRAAK

1834 VDS

Welkom
Welcome
Willkomm

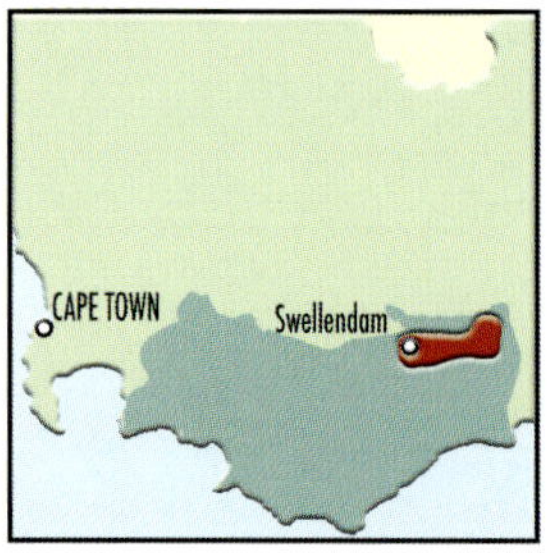

When Alan Paton wrote, 'Ah, but your land is beautiful', he might have had this corner of the Overberg in mind. It's a farmer's dream and a painter's paradise, with vistas of imposing mountains, rolling hills, hidden kloofs and white-washed cottages in unbearably beautiful settings. And no month is the same, as each season marks its changes on the surrounding landscape.

The elegance of Swellendam

Swellendam is a beautiful town with many stunning old houses and an extremely colourful history. Back in the early days when pioneering men were setting off to farm in the wilderness beneath the Langeberg Mountains, the Dutch East India Company realised it needed to establish a third magisterial district far from Cape Town. Although it was easily possible to keep an eye on settlers in nearby towns such as Stellenbosch and Franschhoek, they were battling to keep track of the burghers who had headed off into the interior to farm and, amongst other offences, omitted to pay any rent that was due to the Company. So, after some deliberation, a spot was chosen on the banks of the Cornlands River and, in 1746, the Company started building the Drostdy. The *dorp*, with its dusty, wagon-rutted streets was soon named Swellendam after the Dutch governor, Hendrik Swellengrebel, and his wife Helena ten Damme. This easternmost settlement on the Ou Kaapse Wapad, the main wagon route into the interior, was where everyone stopped to stock up on provisions before setting off for the treacherous journey inland.

The burghers were an unruly bunch and, in the late 1790s, they expressed their dissatisfaction with the *landdrost* by forcing him to resign. For three months Swellendam became a republic, headed up by Hermanus Steyn, but any plans for an extended rule came to an end when the British took occupation of the Cape. According to a local farmer, one of the issues that had got the burghers' ire up was the challenge to their existing right to catch single Khoekhoen and San women and make them the property of the farmer for life.

Today, Swellendam has lost some of the Wild West spirit that once made it such a rollicking place and it now serves as a commercial centre for local grain and sheep farmers.

The town is home to a wide variety of traditional South African architectural styles. There are elegant gables, imposing front doors, half-hipped roofs and vine-covered verandas – a distinctive feature of Cape architecture. Spend time wandering around the town and, before long, you'll be able to identify which buildings are Cape Dutch, Cape Georgian, Cape Edwardian or Late Victorian. Just for pointers: the Drostdy (2 Drostdy Street) is Cape Dutch; Mayville House (4 Hermanus Steyn Street) is Cape Dutch/Cape Georgian; 8 Hermanus Steyn Street is Late Victorian, while 11 Van Oudtshoorn Road is Cape Edwardian. Just to confuse you even further, the old St Luke's Church building (72 Voortrek Street) is Cape Gothic!

The craftsmanship of local Malay masons and plasterers is evident on many buildings in and around Swellendam, particularly in the moulded plasterwork on the gables. Higi Hendricks was the head of the Malay family who lived in Swellendam from 1860 to 1886. He became the well-known spiritual leader of the local Malay community, who were mostly artisans in the building trade.

Some of the architectural features of the Dutch Reformed Church, such as the minaret-type tower and the onion-shaped dome, clearly show their influence, as does the plasterwork on the wine cellar at the Drostdy. However, when this plasterwork went out of fashion in the *platteland*, most of the artisans moved back to Cape Town. Mr Hendricks sent his four sons to Mecca and one of them, Mohammed Salie, born in 1869, returned to Cape Town as the first qualified Sheikh and founder of the Cape Town Mosque.

Bontebok National Park

When settlers first arrived in the Cape Colony, they had little regard for the animals that teemed in the grasslands. Like so many other species, the bontebok (*Damaliscus dorcas dorcas*), with its wonderful coat of brown, white and glossy black, became fair game. In 1689 a settler noted in his journal that he had seen a herd of around 1 000 bontebok racing on the rolling hills just beyond Bot River. But old photos illustrate graphically what happened to the antelope as hunting parties shot them within a hair's breadth of extinction. In 1803 herds of as few as 10 antelope remained and by 1927 the numbers had dwindled so dramatically that there were just over 100 remaining in and around Bredasdorp and Swellendam.

In 1960 the Bontebok National Park was proclaimed near Swellendam. The small remaining herd of 84 animals was transported there in that year but only 61 survived the move. Fortunately, by 1962 the numbers had recovered to 84 and each year they continue to swell.

The Coachman
Guest House
Bed & Breakfast
Luxury Garden Suites
Salt Water Pool

DISCOM DISCOM DISCOM

OPENING SPREAD: The Hermitage Valley, Swellendam, and other scenes from the region. PREVIOUS SPREAD CLOCKWISE FROM TOP LEFT: The Coachman Guest House in Swellendam; Wildebraam Youngberry Farm produces liqueurs and other berry products; Swellendam village street; Dutch Reformed Church, Swellendam.
THIS PAGE CLOCKWISE FROM TOP LEFT: The Overberg is famous for its merino wool; simple farm cottages, like this one on the N2 near Swellendam, dot the region; the Bontebok National Park was established 40 years ago (see p158); pick your own berries at Wildebraam (see p173); Tradouw Guest House, Barrydale. OPPOSITE CLOCKWISE FROM TOP LEFT: A ploughman prepares the land at Zuurbraak; a tranquil dam near Swellendam; the peaceful Hermitage Valley; San model, Swellendam museum complex (see p173); country house, Barrydale.

Two small villages

En route to Swellendam on the N2, be sure to stop off in Riviersonderend and Stormsvlei. When the first explorers to come across the river flowing eastwards from its source in the mighty Hottentots Holland Mountains, it seemed to stretch forever and 'without end', which explains the origin of the name of the Sonderend River, the town, as well as the mountain range (see p145). Riviersonderend is typical of many South African farming towns: there's the imposing church, astonishing rose bushes that seem to grow effortlessly and the farmer's co-op. On Sundays, everyone closes shop and you'll find dusty *bakkies* jostling for parking outside the church. Stormsvlei, on the other hand, is like something out of a picture book – a tiny hamlet perched on the edge of the Sonderend River. Although the N2 whisks you past in the blink of an eye, Stormsvlei used to be an important outpost on the Old Cape Wagon Route that linked the Mother City with the interior. After years of neglect, the village is being spruced up and has some good examples of Victorian architecture.

Barrydale

Like every small town in the Overberg, Barrydale is bristling with real *characters*. Not just everyday, *gewone mense*, but larger-than-life individuals who make their mark and are impossible to ignore.

For sure, there are some quieter country folk but for the most part Barrydalers are bigger, louder, more creative and more eccentric than most. A couple of residents have suggested it's because of the water. 'Drink it, and you're gone,' they say ominously. 'The water here makes people mad as hatters!'

But, if you don't go along with that theory, perhaps it has something to do with the town's remarkable location, ringed as it is by the Langeberg Mountains which, according to a few, lend it a certain mystical air. You only have to spend some time in the village to know that it is a cut above most other *dorpies* in the area. It certainly is beautiful and the late afternoon light transforms the rugged landscape into a palette of pinks and golds.

The town sprang up in 1880 around *nagmaal* or the Sacrament of Holy Communion, which happened just four times a year. In the days of ox wagons and horse carts, there was no such thing as a quick trip into town and, because the farms were so spread out, farmers from the outlying districts built small cottages or *nagmaalhuisies* where they would stay while they attended church and caught up on local gossip from their distant neighbours. And, when the first school opened its doors in 1885, the farmers' children were sent to town for the term to stay in the small cottages while they learnt to read and write.

It's a foregone conclusion that the town was named after Joseph Barry – an entrepreneur whose business empire stretched from the coast at Port Beaufort, near Witsand, into the Klein Karoo and Overberg – although he never actually lived in the village (see p178). Although farmers in the area have traditionally focused on producing fruit and sheep, Barrydale didn't escape the ostrich boom, and subsequent bust, which crippled larger towns such as Oudtshoorn.

Today Barrydale is shaking off its sleepy, conservative image as an agricultural and religious outpost. There are still splashes of rural bliss: every second house has a couple of sheep in the back yard; somebody's olive trees on the hill are looking good after the first rain in ages; and there's a notice outside the supermarket offering an excellent breeding ewe and a ram that delivers the goods every time.

But there are also hints (some obvious and some less so) of a different Barrydale. Innovative Cape Town architect Etienne Bruwer from Greenhaus Architects has built two astonishing houses and a wine cellar in the middle of the *dorp*, which suggests that the town will never be the same again. After all, these are houses that are bound to be featured in international architectural magazines and lusted over by those in the know. Instead of the regulation Cape vernacular style, he's opted for rustic local materials and an organic design that blends beautifully with the rural environment.

And, just as practical fly screens are being replaced on the country cottages, so is the clientele at the Barrydale Private Hotel. In place of dusty *bakkies*, there are now black BMWs and shiny Mercedes Benz convertibles. And, instead of beefy farmers with deep tans from days spent in the sun, there are polished couples in tight T-shirts and designer jeans.

Terri Williams, a self proclaimed Jam Tart, is a well-known Barrydale personality. Outspoken and energetic, Terri has her fans – as well as her detractors. But it's like water off a duck's back. This is a small town, after all, and Terri knows very well that people like to have something to talk about. 'Sometimes, just for the hell of it, I start a story and see how it comes back to me,' says Terri mischievously. 'You won't believe the tales people make up! I'm also fighting with old whatshisname at the moment,' she says with a dismissive wave of her hand. 'But, we'll get over it and next month we'll have found a common enemy and will be friends again! The thing about Barrydale is that everyone has a strong opinion so egos are bound to clash.'

Having completed a stint as a chef in London, Terri moved to the countryside ten years ago with her partner, artist Joan Peters. 'I was astonished by how much fruit there was in the town, so we started a jam factory which we called the Jam Tarts and at the same time we opened one of the town's first B&Bs,' Terri explains. 'When we moved here people were a bit suspicious of us and there were lots of rumours circulating about two women opening a guest house. Our name also got people talking and it didn't take long for some to jump to all sorts of conclusions.

'At the time I was friendly with the local *dominee* who rented land from me to graze his horses. The burly farmers at the co-op were used to seeing me coming and going while we were building and one day when I went to buy some supplies they had a go at me, wanting to know if I was running a brothel. The *dominee* had paid me that morning for the grazing and I happened to have his cheque in my back pocket, so without really thinking, I hauled out his cheque, slammed it down on the counter and said something like, "Yes, and I've just had my first customer!" That certainly shut them up and nobody every called the B&B a brothel again.'

For all its charm and quirkiness, though, Barrydale is still beset by the standard small town problems of poverty, unemployment and alcoholism.

Smitsville is the official title for the coloured township behind the town, but, says Terri, it was also known as Steek My Weg (Hide Me Away). The other Jam Tarts, Mina Plaatjies and Suzanna Ben, confirm that life in Barrydale can be excruciatingly hard. It's not uncommon for people to have up to 12 children and the financial burden of this is overwhelming, especially when work is scarce and seasonal. And, if there's a bad year, things get tougher than before.

THIS PAGE: Scenes from Barrydale, which is on the border of the Overberg and the Little Karoo.
OVERLEAF: A characterful old farmhouse in the Barrydale area.

It's also not unusual for children to go to school for only a couple of years, and then leave to look for work and help support their younger siblings.

'I am friendly with a tour guide who brings German tourists to Barrydale,' continues Terri. 'When people come here they are struck both by the town's beauty and the poverty and they always ask what they can do, so I suggest that they bring two suitcases with them on holiday – one for their belongings and the other for clothes and toys they're prepared to give away. That way they can shop in South Africa and have a spare suitcase to take all their stuff home in, and we are able to provide families in need with clothes and toys they would never otherwise be able to afford.'

While life in this area on the edge of the Karoo has a hard edge to it, however, there is reason for hope. John Nortje is the Community Development Manager for the Swellendam Municipality. Smitsville and Barrydale, with a collective population of between 3 000 and 4 000 inhabitants, fall under his jurisdiction.

'There is a housing project on the go that will provide around 150 new houses to the people of the area, and a number of poverty alleviation projects are being started. There is also a farming project, as well as talk about specialising in growing chillies. We want to stimulate entrepreneurship here so that the community can start uplifting itself.'

There's a photostatted note in Die Wit Huis where Terri and the Jam Tarts sell their wares and serve breakfast and lunch. It reads:

Damhoek Cheese

This is not a 'cute' little blurb about how romantic and fascinating our cheese & 'life on the farm' is.

It's bloody hard work seven days a week and it's taken four years to get the thing to pay for itself. (We still work for love & charity!)

If it wasn't that our eight cows and one bull have replaced our children (we are in our fifties) we would chuck it tomorrow! So please buy more than you can afford so that we can start getting some of our pension back. Our oldest cow, Vensterblom, is also due to go on pension.

PS – The longest our milk stands is from evening milking (sounds romantic) till morn. We do not pasteurise. We do not use pesticides or artificial fertiliser on our feed. We wash our hands regularly.

PPS – We need all the hormones we can get, so the cows get none.

As we said, everyone in Barrydale is a *character.*

Zuurbraak

When you turn off the busy N2 highway and take a short, winding drive along the R324, nothing prepares you for the pretty village of Zuurbraak at the foot of the Tradouw Pass between Swellendam and Barrydale. Before you get there, you pass lush dairy pastures on your left and fields of Brussels sprouts on your right, then down a pretty, forested gorge and you're there – in a proverbial Garden of Eden. It is beautiful, with fertile soil the colour of dark, strong chocolate. Even at the end of a long, dry summer, there's plenty of water and the fields are a tumble of sweet potatoes and green beans.

Over the weekends when, according to residents, the village is 'packed with visitors from the Cape', it still has a somnambulant quality. Everyone strolls about slowly, arm in arm and, as big trucks and cars trundle on noisily by, a horse dozes under a fig tree outside an open front door with five sheep that lie unperturbed at his feet. It's a scene of pastoral bliss and quiet – far removed from the busy N2 crammed with fast cars on the way to distant places.

A Khoekhoen clan, the Attaqua, originally occupied this area, which lies on ancient trade routes. They called their settlement Xairu, which means 'beautiful'. When the earliest Dutch cattle traders started doing business here they didn't have to stretch their imagination when they translated the name to 'Paradise'. In 1809, the tribe's traditional way of life was to change forever when their leader, Hans Moos, invited the London Mission Society to come to the village and spread the word.

The missionaries arrived at the Cape, made the arduous journey to the foot of the Tradouw Pass and liked what they saw. Who couldn't fall in love with this corner of the Cape? In 1812, Zuurbraak became a mission station. Over 60 years later it was taken over by the Algemeende Sending Kerk. Only five years after that a split developed within the congregation and the Anglican Church was established. In a village of just over 2 500 residents, today churches flourish and, apart from the founding churches that were established centuries ago, the village now has three new Pentecostal Churches, as well as one from the New Apostolic order.

There's a quiet pride in the people who have chosen to stay behind in the village rather than look for work in Cape Town or on surrounding farms. There's a productive chair factory in the old school house on top of the hill that makes rustic chairs with seagrass seats, and Piet Botha is busy transforming the unwanted wattle and hakea into whimsical garden furniture which you can't miss as you drive through the town. On a warm autumn morning, Samuel Kayster washes down the carts and feeds his horses that he uses for tourist rides.

'It's a beautiful place to live,' says Samuel with a smile, 'but communities need to work hard to preserve this way of life. Nowadays there are plenty of distractions. Cape Town is a short journey away, but working with animals and on the land is much more satisfying.'

Sitting pretty

The Suurbraak Carpentry Co-op was started in the early 1980s when a group of people decided they needed to earn an income close to home rather than making the lonely trek to the city – and so they hit on the idea of making chairs using the old-fashioned method of bodging. Today the Suurbraak Carpentry Co-op employs three men and three women who use both traditional and modern tools to produce about ten chairs per day. Their products are in much demand throughout South Africa and, chances are, you've sat on one of their chairs at a restaurant.

Mission stations during the nineteenth century were hubs of activity and many of the village residents were expert crafts people. Although many have forgotten these time-honoured crafts, bodging dates back at least 500 years and has its origins in the huge English forests. Skilled carpenters would buy up tree lots and fell the young saplings, which they would then turn into chair legs and parts. They worked with the wood while it was still green, and then stacked the parts to season and dry. When these were done, they would sell the chair legs to factories where the pieces were put together.

There's some debate about how bodgers ended up being called by such a strange name. Some think it could come from the word 'badger' because, like this shy woodland creature, bodgers spent long months in isolation working at their craft, and would only be seen at dusk and dawn when they emerged from their greeny isolation. There's another suggestion that it was the name once given to travelling salesmen – some of whom were bodgers when they weren't on the road – and hence the name eventually came to refer to their second job as well.

Exploring the area

Grootvadersbosch is one of the Cape's least-explored nature reserves and definitely worth discovering by nature lovers. The 250-hectare reserve is established on what used to be a farm called Melkhoutskraal. The owner was known as the Groot Vader (Great Father), although nobody is certain if he got that name from the enormous trees in the area, or because he was a grandfather!

From 1896 to 1913, exotic trees such as Australian blackwoods and Californian redwoods were planted to cover the areas denuded by woodcutters. However, Cape Nature is now working to reclaim these areas for indigenous species such as stinkwood and yellowwood.

An abundant bird life is the reserve's biggest drawcard and forests such as these are hard to find this far south of Knysna. There are two bird hides to escape to and you might be lucky enough to spot the Klaas's cuckoo or the Narina trogon.

Grootvadersbosch borders the Boosmansbos Wilderness Area, which dramatically increases the area you can explore – and lose yourself in. If you're feeling energetic, there's the 58-kilometre Grootvadersbosch Conservancy Cycle Trail that's graded moderate to difficult.

Is it a Z or S?

There's some confusion about whether to spell the village Zuurbraak or Suurbraak. Maggy Jantjies from the Tourism Information Bureau remembers being at school in the 1960s and the teacher announcing that the name had changed and they had to spell it with an S. Although residents have gone along with this folly for decades, they're now reverting to the old Dutch spelling of Zuurbraak. What does the name mean? According to some, it means sour, fallow ground, which is absurd considering how fertile this little valley is.

TOP LEFT AND LEFT: Life in Zuurbraak is unhurried. It's no surprise that the original Khoekhoen clan, the Attaqua, called their settlement Xairu, which means 'beautiful'. Even today the village is truly picturesque and unspoilt. BELOW: The Tradouw Pass is characterised by some dizzying turns and curves and is a feat of engineering (see text left). When the road opened in the early 1870s, life in the area changed dramatically as farmers were able to move their goods more easily from Barrydale to Swellendam and the rest of the Overberg.

The Tradouw Pass

The pass linking Zuurbraak and Barrydale is just one of the 13 passes engineered by master road engineer Thomas Bain – a man with great foresight and respect for nature. He knew that rivers always preferred the path of least resistance and so decided the pass should follow the same route as the Tradouw River that carves its way through the mountain range. The pass was built using convict labour and was completed in 1873. It's believed the word derives from the Hessequa Khoekhoen word meaning 'the way of the women'.

THIS PAGE: Impressions of Zuurbraak, first established as a mission station in 1812 by the London Mission Society (see p166).
OPPOSITE CLOCKWISE FROM LEFT: Mario Sugelaar, Dougie Hendricks, Claire and James Page, Hansie Hendricks and Jacob Hendricks are all residents of this quiet village at the foot of the Tradouw Pass (see p166 and 167). Zuurbraak locals say they happily choose the rural way of life – with all its accompanying hardships – rather than moving to the city in search of other work.

TOP: The famous Granny's Vetkoek shop on Main Road, Swellendam is run by husband-and-wife team Hein and Johannine Binneman. ABOVE: Detail from an old village sign, Zuurbraak.
TOP RIGHT AND OPPOSITE TOP LEFT: Produce from Die Wit Huis, Barrydale. You can stock up on enough preserves and jams to sink a ship and tuck into a simple, wholesome meal.
RIGHT: Try the Tradouw Guest House for real home-from-home hospitality. OPPOSITE BOTTOM LEFT: Swellendam has many characterful shops where visitors can spend hours browsing for country bargains. OPPOSITE BOTTOM RIGHT: Delicious milk tart and fresh bread are baked over the coals at the Swellendam Drostdy Museum.

Apple & chilli chutney

The Jam Tarts are famous for their tomato chilli jam which, like all of their preserves, they have labelled with a saucy drawing of a salacious woman with a come-hither look. Getting the recipe for their signature jam, however, will take brutal methods. Here, instead, is Terri's recipe for apple and chilli chutney with strict instructions from her to make the chutney with love! That way it will taste all the better. This chutney is especially good served with cheese or roast pork.

2 cups brown vinegar
1 cup sugar
1 tbsp grated fresh ginger
4 fresh red chillies, chopped
1 t mustard seeds
2 cups water
4 large apples, peeled and chopped
2 medium onions, chopped

Combine the first six ingredients in a large pot. Heat until the sugar has dissolved and stir in the apples and onions. Bring to the boil, then simmer uncovered, stirring occasionally for about 1 hour or until thick. Pour into hot, clean jars and close tightly. (This should make about 4 jars.) Cool. Turn the jars upside down to create a vacuum. Leave until they are cold and then make your own fancy labels. Of course, if this seems like too much effort, you can always buy some the next time you're in Barrydale.

ABOVE: The towering peaks of the Langeberg in Swellendam are as imposing as they are spectacular. BOTTOM LEFT TO RIGHT: House detail, Swellendam; the fertile Hermitage Valley; Zuurbraak's chair factory still uses the time-honoured tradition of bodging (see p166); picking berries on Wildebraam Farm (see p173).

Favourites

You can't leave the area without ...

- Stopping at the picturesque Stormsvlei with its newly restored buildings (see p161). It's beautiful!
- Spending a morning at the museum complex in Swellendam. Be sure to have a delicious sandwich from the museum café. They use bread baked on the coals in the Ambagswerf (trade yard) behind the museum.
- Admiring the exquisite heritage roses in the garden at Mayville House in Swellendam.
- Picking a bucket of youngberries at the Wildebraam berry farm in the picturesque Hermitage Valley. Just follow the signs for the centre of Swellendam. For the brave, they also have some pretty potent berry liqueurs that deliver a 24 percent alcohol kick.
- Camping in the Bontebok National Park in spring when the flowers are out. The sight of the colourful antelope with the blue mountains in the distance is good for the most wintery weary soul (see p158).
- Taking a guided tour of Zuurbraak (see p166). You can even go on horseback or by horse cart if walking or driving is too tame. Either way, you won't be disappointed as you are bound to meet some of the friendliest people in the Overberg.
- Doing the Grootvadersbosch Conservancy Cycle trail on your mountain bike. It's 58 kilometres through what used to be one of the oldest farms in the area.
- Having tea and a jam tart at Die Wit Huis in Barrydale. You can catch up on local gossip and stock up on the Jam Tarts' famous tomato chilli jam at the same time. Be sure to visit the art gallery at the back (see p162).
- Sitting around a fire on a cold winter's night with some of Barrydale's finest red wines.
- Running your hand over some of the beautiful dry stone walls that are appearing all around Barrydale and wishing you could also have one.
- Investing in some paints or a camera. How can you possibly spend time here without trying to capture the play of light on the fields and mountains?
- Going for an early morning walk around Barrydale before anybody else is up. You'll have the quiet streets to yourself and it's the ideal time to lean over people's fences to see what has been done to renovate the sweet cottages in the town.
- Walking the labyrinth outside Barrydale. By appointment only. If you really want to, you'll find out how ...
- Seeing if you can find the rare protea *Leucadendron tradouwense* – also known as the Tradouw conebush – which is found around the Tradouw Pass (see p166).

Contact numbers

Barrydale Tourism: 028-572-1572
Riviersonderend Tourism: 028-261-1511
Swellendam Tourism: 028-514-2770
Zuurbraak Tourism and guided tours: 028-522-1806

Barrydale Wine Cellar: 028-572-1012
Bontebok National Park: 028-514-2735
Buffeljachts Watersports (Swellendam): 082-826-0121
Die Wit Huis (Barrydale): 028-572-1173
Grootvadersbosch Conservancy Cycle Trail (Barrydale): 028-425-5020 or 028-722-2412
Marloth Nature Reserve (Swellendam): 028-514-1410
Suurbraak Carpentry Co-op: 028-522-1452
Swellendam Drostdy Museum and Mayville House: 028-514-1138
Swellendam Outdoor Adventures: 028-514-3650
Wildebraam Berry Farm (Swellendam): 028-514-2308
Zuurbraak horsecart rides: 028-522-1806

Where to stay

www.overberginfo.com
Barrydale Private Hotel: 028-572-1226
Die Oude Pastorie (Swellendam): 028-514-3016
Jan Harmsgat Country House (near Swellendam): 023-616-3407
Roosje van de Kaap (Swellendam): 028-514-3001
Tradouw Guest House (Barrydale): 028-572-1434

TOP: A lonely farm cottage, Swellendam. ABOVE: The Drostdy Museum has distinctive plasterwork that can be attributed to Malay masons who lived here in the 1800s. RIGHT: Buffeljagsdam, Swellendam. OPPOSITE TOP: Buffeljagsriver, Zuurbraak. OPPOSITE BOTTOM: The Langeberg Mountains, Swellendam.

A long road & a wide river

MALGAS, INFANTA and WITSAND

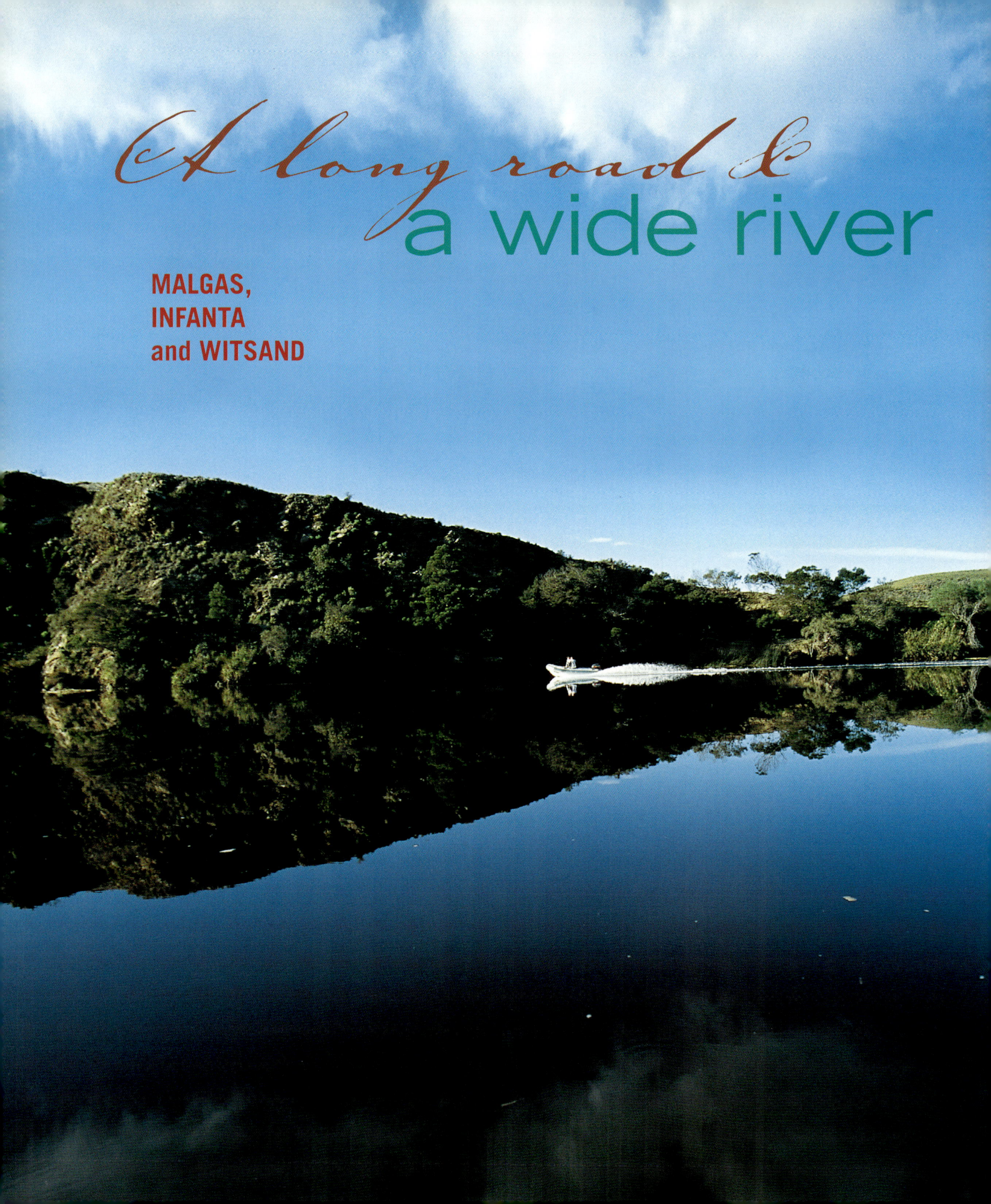

31|5|56

SHOP

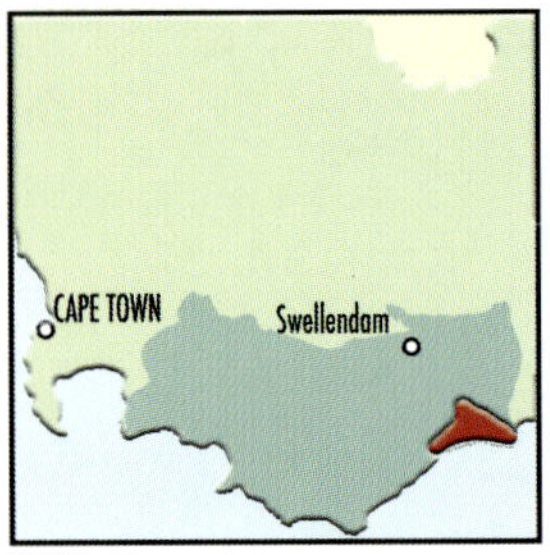

The countryside is all rolling hills and soft curves that turn a muted brown towards the end of summer. The mighty Breede River, with its many moods, dominates this landscape. Languid at times, it can turn into a raging beast within a couple of hours. The river has always exerted a powerful pull over the region — in the early days it was an important avenue of transport, while today its waters are popular for a range of fun activities.

Mysterious Malgas

They say that you can always tell the difference between a local and a visitor by seeing who waves as you fly past each other on dusty country roads. Convention has it that locals always wave because they're friendly and welcoming, but the Malgas–Infanta route seems to be an exception to this rule. A few men in *bakkies* might lift a finger, but mostly they keep their hands firmly gripped on their steering wheels. Probably for good reason as the condition of the road is less than ideal: rutted, full of potholes and with stinging stones that ricochet off your windshield.

This road has always been a talking point and there seem to be two camps on the subject: those who want the road repaired (or, better still, tarred) and those who want it to stay just as it is. The reasoning is simple: the more fearsome the road, the fewer people will be tempted to make the journey. And, for some, that means more peace and quiet – exactly why they came to live here in the first place. There was a time when the Swellendam–Infanta run took a good three hours, and in the beginning you had to stop to open over 100 farm gates!

Although getting there is faster than before, during the week Malgas – first named Malagaskraal by the Dutch after the Khoekhoen chief who originally settled on the banks of the Breede River – certainly is quiet. It's so quiet, in fact, that there's a slow, sunned-up puff adder lying in the middle of road. It's going nowhere because it doesn't need to. When the snake finally moves off, it's followed closely by a swift mongoose.

There are just a handful of permanent residents in the hamlet and, unless you make a concerted effort, it's easy to miss them almost entirely. One old man who was born and bred here still goes down to the pont everyday in his *bakkie* to sit in the shade of the blue gum trees and watch the comings and goings across the river. You can tell a lot about people by just watching what they do: who has a new car (business must be good), whose kids are growing (off to weekly boarding school on a Monday morning and back on a Friday afternoon) and who's getting restless (too many trips to the city).

Malgas isn't just one place, it's a series of little settlements strung out like pearls on the water's edge: Brakfontein, Malgas, Lemoentuin, Matjieskloof, Diep Kloof and Breede Riverine. Malgas is 35 kilometres from the mouth of the Breede River but the river is tidal for up to 60 kilometres, so don't be surprised if you're relaxing on its banks, only to see what appears to be the river flowing languidly upstream. Depending on conditions, the water can also be salty up to 20 kilometres from the river mouth.

The old packing sheds, canteens and settler cottages here are testimony to a time when the Breede River played an important role in the economic development of the Overberg and boats chugged up and down the river delivering much needed cargo from Port Beaufort, then a thriving port near Witsand. Because travel into the interior along bumpy wagon tracks was so arduous, going by sea seemed like the perfect solution and the Breede River appeared to be the answer to every entrepreneur's dream.

A tale of two towns

An old Overberg name, Benjamin Moodie, initially built a store and set up the shipping route between Port Beaufort and Cape Town, but the farmers of the area were wary because of the economic risk involved. Goods lost at sea were their financial responsibility and it wasn't a chance many of them were prepared to take.

In 1822 the people of the Swellendam district were left destitute by drought and blight, and the government undertook to supply them with rice and grain to tide them over. When the authorities in Cape Town called for transport tenders, the entrepreneur Joseph Barry confounded his competitors by chartering a boat as far as Port Beaufort, and then transporting the food by horse and cart from there to Swellendam. He also took along other much-needed goods, which the settlers in the area quickly snapped up.

Barry soon found an untapped market and his business began to flourish. In 1823 he opened a small trading store in Port Beaufort and starting transporting grain and wool from the area back to the Cape. He began buying produce from the farmers – which he then exported himself – and also had the government contract to deliver the mail to the area.

For a time, there seemed no stopping this innovative businessman and his partners and they put up buildings at

PREVIOUS SPREAD: Power boating at Lemoentuin on the Breede River and other scenes from the region. RIGHT: Entrance to the general dealer in Malgas, the only supply store in this tiny hamlet. FAR RIGHT: The church at Malgas has a clear watermark halfway up its walls from when the river broke its banks and flooded the area in 2003. BELOW: One of Marthinus Fouché's (see p180) historical photographs of the pont at Malgas showing Moxie Dunn (on the right) at work. CENTRE RIGHT: Inside the Malgas general dealer, where visitors and residents stock up on basic household items. BOTTOM: The modern-day pont has been in operation since 1952 (see text box below).

Malgas Pont

Not only is the Malgas pont legendary, but so is Moxie Dunn, the man who worked the pont by himself for several decades. Moxie started out as a farmer and, when he retired in 1961, he was asked to keep an eye on the pont for a few days. Those few days turned into 30 years and, before Moxie hurt his foot towards the end of his career, he never missed a day's work in his life. The pont was first used in 1860 and the present model has been in operation since 1952.

Port Beaufort and Swellendam to manage the goods they handled. Because the Barrys were related to the big sheep farmers of the area, they also needed to find a quick way of exporting the wool that was being grown on farms in the district and so, 35 kilometres up the river at Malgas, they built warehouses, a wool store, a hotel and canteen. There was even a church and a pont (see p179).

Central to their success was the *Kadie*, the steamer Barry & Nephews had especially built to cope with the hazards of the Breede River. This little port was inaccessible to bigger steamers and so the *Kadie*'s fate and the history of Malgas and Port Beaufort are integrally interwoven.

When the *Kadie* ran aground on a sandbar in the Breede River in 1865, it was one of two bruising blows in that year for the Barry empire – the other being a fire that had swept through their stores in Swellendam. The loss of the *Kadie* didn't only have serious consequences for the Barrys, but also had a profound effect on the whole area. *The Cape Argus* reported at the time:

> *The brave little* Kadie *has at last laid her bones on the South African shores. We have been so accustomed to see the plucky little craft with her red cutwater come in and out of the bay, that it is difficult to believe that she will not appear again.*

Over the years, the roads inland had improved enormously and the desperate need for sea travel as a way of accessing the outside world had gradually fallen away. But, sadly, when Barry & Nephews crumbled, the company still took the fortunes of many Overberg farmers with it. In his book *Overberg Outspan – A Chronicle of People and Places in the South Western Districts of the Cape*, Edmund H. Burrows explains:

> *Prominent farmers were ruined by pledging themselves beyond their means as security for an enterprise they were convinced could never fail. More fortunate victims sold a triangular wedge of land out of their beautiful round farms they had inherited from their fathers, which had been measured out on horseback from the* opstal *in the centre. Some of the places are still to be seen on surveyors' charts, their circular form disturbed by the missing Barry* se hoek*' which was lopped off at the time of the* groot bankrotskap.

Although Port Beaufort only flourished as a port until the late 1860s when the Barry empire tragically collapsed, today it is a great place to escape on holiday. The mouth of the Breede River is South Africa's richest fishing estuary and the area also offers people exceptional watching and birding opportunities. The old customs house is now an inn and the Barry Church, which was completed by Thomas Barry in 1849, is a National Monument.

Photographs of the past

Marthinus Fouché is a *ware* Overberger. He was born in Malgas and lives in a caravan on a hill overlooking the river. Time moves too slowly for 76-year-old Marthinus and he wishes he had more books to help pass the time.

If he doesn't have books, then Marthinus certainly has photographs of Malgas from way back. There's a photo of the original pont with an enormous wagon and a span of at least six mules pulling the load. The pont also has a ship's wheel in the middle but it's difficult to establish what it was used for. What the photos do capture, though, is just how agrarian the community was. There's Marthinus's father standing with a gun and a brace of wild birds that he's shot; a flock of sheep with their shepherd and his dog on the pont; and only later a smart car and people dressed, not for work, but leisure.

Marthinus's photographs also capture him as a good looking young man and – even earlier still – as a very small boy *kaalvoet* and in shorts. There's a picture of a woman milking a cow, and of somebody tall and striking standing next to a group of horses.

'That was my mother,' says Marthinus slowly. 'She liked to work outside and could match any man. She ploughed, sowed, harvested and worked with the horses. Here's a photo of me as a child when she taught me to ride. But, even though she preferred to be outside a lot, she also sewed beautifully.'

These days Marthinus walks cautiously. His leg is sore, but his mind is sharp. He reels off dates of events – both local and international – and can tell you when which ships went down and what happened during the flood. He likes discussing these things with Johannes Kemp – another old-timer and a good companion to shoot the breeze with.

Johannes isn't at home, but he's easy to find at the crossroads near the store. His grandparents first settled here in 1856 and he knows the curves of the hills and road as well as the back of his hand. He remembers the time when people used to tap the aloes in the area for their sap.

'It's medicinal and used for lots of different things,' he explains (see p186). Today, like most days, Johannes is waiting for his granddaughters to be dropped off after school. He's sitting in his *bakkie* with his youngest grandchild, a blonde slip of a child who is restless and lies on the seat with her feet on the window or sits in the open window swinging her legs. She might be wriggly, but she knows her manners and wouldn't dare interrupt *oupa* while he's talking to other people. All it takes from him is one quiet word and she curls up on the front seat like a kitten in the sun.

Sometimes Johannes has to wait a couple of hours if the lift is late but it doesn't really matter – it gives him time to doze, look at the hills in the distance and smoke his pipe.

When the two girls Old Man Kemp is waiting for get dropped off, they kiss *oupa* hello and squeeze into the front of the *bakkie*. They've still got their school uniforms on but their shoes are already off for the rest of the day.

LEFT: Private holiday homes, most with their own jetties and powerboats, hug the river banks between Lemoentuin and Breede Riverine.
BELOW: Wakeboarding on the Breede River close to the Tides River Lodge near Malgas. The Breede River is also known for its safe swimming, and excellent waterskiing, kayaking and tubing opportunities.

Old names and the Dunn daughters

The Breede River Valley is dominated by old family names that have helped shape the region. You can't take a step without meeting a Dunn, a Van As, a Moodie or an Uys – or several of them at once. Things get complicated because, one elderly Dunn descendent explained, 'back in those days nobody had transport so you all ended up marrying people in the district. It wasn't uncommon for two brothers to marry two sisters.' Or, and this is where you have to watch out, for a brother and a sister to marry a brother and a sister. So, chances are you will come across a Dunn man married to a Van As woman, while the Van As brother might be married to the Dunn sister. The best advice is simple: be polite to everybody and don't say anything nasty about somebody in front of anybody you don't know well. They might have different surnames, but, for all you know, they could be family.

Every family has its own history, but the story about William Dunn and his daughters has had people talking for well over a century. Dunn arrived in San Sebastian's Bay in 1828 where he served as a government official, ensuring that smuggling didn't take place and assisting in preventing any mutinies that were brewing. Over time he acquired a vast tract of land at Cape Infanta on the opposite side of the Breede River. Nobody is entirely sure what attracted him to this stretch. It was inhospitable, wild and isolated. Dunn had six children – three sons and three daughters – but the girls never married and lived out their days at the family's Rietfontein homestead.

There are whispers that the three women became increasingly eccentric and that trunks of elaborate clothes would arrive for them from London while the house was falling apart around them. There are also accounts of the women wearing expensive ball gowns with their *velskoene* and eating ever-diminishing meals off expensive imported cutlery and crockery. You can only begin to imagine why the daughters never married and what kept them in these moments of increasing madness. Too much wind and too many silent hours can play havoc with a person's mind. Towards the end of their lives they composed a letter to the customs official at Port Beaufort, complaining about a madman who was disturbing them. Sarah Dunn wrote:

> *We the undersigned have to lay a request before the administration of Justice and of Her Majesty's Laws in this Colony. We have for a long time paid Taxes for the support of Government and now we have need to demand Protection, for where Allegiance is faithful, Protection is to be claimed...'*
>
> (From *Overberg Outspan* by Edmund H. Burrows.)

Fishing on the Breede

Pack your oilskins – this is fishing territory where people spend their days on the river or a boat with a fishing rod in their hand. The big thing used to be becoming a member of the 100-pound Club, which meant catching a kabeljou of 50 kilograms or more. Things have shifted, though, as the more savvy fishermen have realised that hauling huge fish out comes at an enormous environmental cost that just isn't worth the photo and round of beers afterwards. Now, with growing interest in the Lower Breede River Conservancy (see opposite), fishermen are choosing rather to tag and release. This is the deal: chuck back anything smaller than 50 centimetres and keep anything under 120 centimetres. Anything over 120 centimetres goes straight back, as this is the breeding stock you want to leave behind so that your children have something to look forward to. When you're not hunting the mighty kabeljou, the fish you're likely to find are grunter, steenbras, leervis and elf.

TOP: Holiday homes at Malgas. ABOVE AND RIGHT: The Bush Pub is great for sundowners. MIDDLE: To catch and prepare your own fish is a pleasure of life on the Breede. FAR RIGHT (from top to bottom): You might catch grunter, harder, kabeljou or zebra fish. OPPOSITE: Five hundred metres of tar break the monotony of the gravel road between Malgas and Breede Riverine.

Conservation on the river

The Lower Breede River Conservancy was formed in 1996 and, together with local authorities, manages the lower reaches of the river. Its biggest problems are the rampant water hyacinth, greedy property developers who disregard regulations, and poachers who use nets to plunder the river.

The water hyacinth (*Eichhornia crassipes*) is an ongoing headache. It originated in South America but has become naturalised in many warm areas of the world including Central America, Africa, India and Australia. It's considered one of the most productive plants on earth – but this isn't a good thing. The water hyacinth's prolific growth has a disastrous impact on rivers and inland lakes, as it stops other indigenous water plants from growing and lowers the oxygen levels of the water beneath the thick mats that it forms. As if that's not bad enough, the hyacinth is also an excellent breeding ground for mosquitoes.

The Lower Breede River Conservancy works closely with conservation authorities to keep the pesky weed under control by using an approved herbicide and releasing beetles – part of the weevil family – into the water.

Indigenous vegetation

Although most of the fertile Overberg region has been cultivated for farming, look out for the few remaining patches of *renosterveld*, which you'll usually find in the parts of valleys that tractors and harvesters can't get to – or on areas given over to conservation.

Renosterveld is dominated by members of the daisy family (*Asteraceae*) and is also often referred to as *renosterbos* – or rhinoceros bush – after one of the dominant species, *Elytropappus rhinocerotis*.

There's some debate about the origin of the name, however, and some people believe it came from the black rhino that once used to graze on it, while others think it is the grey shrub's resemblance to the tough hide of the rhinoceros that gave rise to the name.

Renosterveld vegetation is incredibly diverse and plentiful and contains 1 036 species of daisy, 760 species of pea, 661 species of iris, 418 species of snapdragon, 227 species of orchid and 660 species of *vygie*. Grasses are also abundant within this vegetation type.

Their fiery fingers cut a colourful swathe as far as the eye can see ...

ABOVE: *Aloe ferox* is one of the plant species found in the patches of *renosterveld* between farms. Its sap has medicinal and cosmetic uses (see p186).
RIGHT AND OVERLEAF TOP: Ostrich farms line the dirt road between Malgas and Swellendam.
OPPOSITE: Scenes from De Hoop Nature Reserve: Dune fynbos is found close to the coast, while limestone fynbos is typical further inland and includes the protea, erica and restio families. Angulate tortoises are commonly seen on the reserve's roads, especially when rainy weather's on the way. There are around 300 bontebok roaming the reserve, and rock agamas are generally found in the more rocky habitats.

Renosterbos and some other *renosterveld* species have tiny leaves coated with a waxy substance that helps reduce water loss. It burns well, even when green, and has therefore often been used for fuel. *Renosterbos* is also used medicinally to cure flu and typhoid.

The fact that *renosterveld* typically grows on fertile soil has largely been its downfall, as most of these areas have been ploughed for farming. Unfortunately, less than 10 percent of *renosterveld* is left and most of this is on private land.

The red and orange aloe flowers are an integral part of the Breede River landscape. Come autumn, their fiery fingers cut a colourful swathe as far as the eye can see. Although people stopped tapping aloes in this area a long time ago, in other parts of southern Cape this is a multi-million rand industry and each year hundreds of aloe tappers trudge through the veld collecting the precious sap from the bitter aloe, or *Aloe ferox*.

The sap that is drained in the fields is known as bitter sap and is cooked down to form crystals. Amongst other things, these crystals are added to animal feed and water, as they serve as a powerful repellent against ticks, fleas and flies. The leaves are then taken back to the factory where they are processed for use in the pharmaceutical and cosmetic industry, and 80 percent of these products are exported.

The bitter skin is also removed, leaving behind what's known as the aloe 'fillet'. This is cubed and added to yoghurt, chutneys, jams, sweets and used as a dried fruit. Very healthy! According to old wives' tales, aloes are excellent for treating everything from digestive disorders to skin problems. They are high in fibre and minerals, especially potassium and calcium. And the bitter juice rubbed onto bitten fingernails is a potent repellent to quit biting.

Back to nature

De Hoop Nature Reserve and Marine Protected Area has been described as the 'Jewel of the Western Cape' and, when the hills are covered in golds, greens and magentas in spring-time, it's as though a magical Persian carpet has landed next to the sea.

The nature reserve takes its name from one of the earliest farms in the area, a horse stud called Hope Farm. It was proclaimed a reserve in 1957 and was used for the breeding of animals such as the bontebok and Cape mountain zebra.

The reserve is extensive – there are 36 000 hectares and unspoilt tracts of indigenous lowland and coastal *fynbos*. It's estimated that 1 500 of the approximately 8 500 species in the Cape Floral Kingdom are found here. In order to provide even greater protection to a wide variety of species, in 1986 a marine protected area stretching five kilometres out to sea was declared. The snorkelling off the coast is superb and, each year from about May to October, southern right whales come to these warmer waters to mate and calve. De Hoop is also home to the last breeding colony of rare Cape vultures in the southwestern Cape.

There are a number of energetic ways to enjoy this spectacular stretch of the Overberg. Choose one of the many mountain bike routes and scenic drives (booking is essential for the De Hoop Mountain Bike Trail). You can also do one of the beautiful day hikes, amongst which are the Vlei, Coastal, Potberg and Klipspringer trails.

The five-day, 54-kilometre Whale Trail is popular for its stunning sea views and sandstone formations, dolphin and whale sightings in season, as well as great swimming and snorkelling in the rock pools. The overnight accommodation in luxury cottages is excellent – although it's also possible to camp – and there's a portage facility too!

RIGHT: Dunes at Koppie Alleen in the De Hoop Nature Reserve. MIDDLE: A characterful outbuilding found on the original farm at Potberg in the De Hoop Nature Reserve. FAR RIGHT: The Whale Trail has become one of the most popular hiking routes in South Africa (see text above).

For the birds

The road from Malgas to Witsand takes you through ostrich countryside. You can't ignore these peculiar looking birds prowling up and down, or the beautiful, arching feathers caught on the barbed wire fences. The contrast between the hard veld and the delicate white feathers is astonishing – and just another one of those South African contradictions that burn a mark on your mind's eye.

Waterkloof Guest House is one of the oldest farms in the area and dates back to the 1700s when the Uys family immigrated from northern Germany. It's been in the family for seven generations and, although initially the family farmed sheep, they've also branched out into ostrich farming and currently have over 3 000 birds. The industry has been in a state of flux in recent years. The strengthening rand has had a negative impact, but then the increase in the incidence of avian flu and mad cow disease has seen an enormous demand for ostrich meat on the overseas markets.

It's not only ostrich meat that's good for you, but the eggs also make for good eating, explains Christine Uys. One ostrich egg equals 24 chicken eggs, but it's lower in cholesterol and brilliant to bake with because the ratio of egg white to yolk is higher so you get a much fluffier and lighter mix.

Christine has been cooking with ostrich for years. Below is one of her favourite recipes, and one that she often serves to her guests.

'If you're preparing ostrich,' Christine explains, 'your best bet is to treat it like game and use the same spices that you would if you were seasoning venison, for instance. One really quick recipe is to marinate ostrich steaks for about a day in a bottle of Greek salad dressing that you can buy from any supermarket. That works really well.'

Infanta

Manuel de Mesquita Perestrello was a Portuguese navigator who in 1575 he worked his way around Africa looking for safe places to sit out the dangerous storms that he knew had previously sunk many ships in these dangerous waters. When Perestrello reached the bay at the mouth of the Breede River, he was overwhelmed by its beauty and the natural resources he found there. Abundant fish and fresh water were what every sailor would have been looking for in those days. He named the bay San Sebastian's Bay after Dom Sebastião, the King of Portugal, and decided to call the west bank of the river 'Infanta'.

Infanta – on the west side of the Breede Estuary (Witsand and Port Beaufort are on the east side) – is still the wild child of the Overstrand. It started its life as a sought-after holiday destination in the early 1900s as just a rough campsite, when there were only a few stone cottages and fishing shacks. These days it's still a bit of a mishmash, but Infanta residents like it that way – rough-and-ready with few pretences. This is the place they come to kick back and slip into their worn beach gear that's frayed at the edges but as comfortable as a kid glove. It's the time to fish, swim, lie in the sun or doze under the milkwoods that have been standing there for as long as anyone can remember. Infanta's also known for its deep sea, river and shore angling, as well as fantastic river and coastal recreation such as windsurfing, skiing and sailing.

Eric Louw's dad was one of the first Infanta residents. The Louws, the Retiefs, the Tolmies and the Hoeks were the advance guard – the adventurous families who staked their claim before having a beach cottage was a fashionable thing to do. The Retief family has a wonderful scrapbook chronicling the families' beach holidays. It's the kind of

Waterkloof ostrich bake

Put your meat in an oven dish and spice it with a ready mix of barbeque or steak and chops spices. Add a few cloves and a little salt and pepper. Open a tin of onion and tomato mix, stir in one tablespoon of sugar and pour that over the meat. Cover the meat well with tinfoil or a tightly fitting lid and cook at 180°C for two hours. Take the meat out and shake over a packet of oxtail soup you make in a cup. This will help thicken the gravy. You can also use regular soup powder but you need to mix this with a little water before adding to your dish. How much of regular mix you use will depend on the amount of meat you're cooking, but expect to use between ½ and 1 packet of soup mix. Return the meat to the dish, cover again and cook for another hour. The secret is to keep the moisture in the dish and, after 3 hours of slow cooking, the meat will be extremely tender and should just fall apart. You can serve this with rice and a fresh salad. For some reason, tomato always takes away the 'gameness' of the meat. If you're really lucky, you might get offered an Overberg lager to go with your meal. It's not available commercially, but apparently the breweries deliver it to the farmers who supply them with the grains they need for their brew.

memoir every family should have. It's nostalgic and captures the kind of blissful summers we all long for. Pasted into the book is an essay Eric wrote.

He was about 12 years old when his dad first bought an Infanta plot. He is now in his golden years, but his mind is as sharp as a needle and he has no problem remembering the paradise of his youth. This is how he describes the holidays of his childhood:

> *Initially there were only five stone houses. The township developed very slowly due, no doubt, to the roughness and winding of the dirt road up and down the steep Ruggens. It took our family approximately three hours to get to Infanta from Swellendam in our Dodge Tourer Motor.*
>
> *We were a comic sight on the road, with running board carriers stacked with food tins, sacks, boxes and a rear carrier similarly loaded with a wire net meat and perishables 'safe' precariously perched thereon and secured by ropes attached to the rear door handles. To complete the circus of our departure for three weeks' heavenly holiday at Infanta, the spaces between the mudguards and the engine cover carried a grain bag with poultry heads pulled through holes cut out of the sacks. There were ducks one side and chickens the other side. In addition, Dad's pointer dog found himself a perch with his forepaws on the poultry bag and hind legs on whatever was on the end of the running board, driver's side.*
>
> *This exodus was the form ever since Dad acquired a car a year or two after the house was completed and we required all that made up the load because our mother ran an excellent dinner table. We ate fish at least once a day and often twice as we became avid rock fishermen and we appreciated the fresh harvest from the sea. In the early years of the 'camp', as we called it, the place saw*

RIGHT: Holiday homes at Infanta on the west side of the Breede River Estuary. MIDDLE: Textures in the dunes at Infanta. FAR RIGHT: View of Witsand from Infanta, on the opposite side of the river.
TOP: Sunset at Infanta, which was given its name in the sixteenth century by Manuel de Mesquita Perestrello (see p187).

visitors as well as occupiers as all families invited guests at Christmas and Easter times.

There were the Rams, the Van Eedens, the Kelloways from Cape Town and a few more who related so well to the Infanta people that they became regulars. The grown-ups were a rare lot and they had a whale of a time on fishing trips in the heavy rowboat of Mr Retief who ruled his crew with an iron hand. These sturdy men rowed across the bay to Takheining, Blombos, Duivenhoks Mouth and back, bringing a marvellous haul of various fish with them. At other times they rounded the Point to beyond Driegaaitjies, to Stilbaaitjie and Uiterstepunt, and brought back cob, stumpnose, musselcracker and red roman of record size. At all times the catch was shared with all and sundry in the camp who wanted fish.

The simple life could not be maintained as more and more stand owners felt the need for a seaside 'shack'. Newcomers came and were viewed with hesitation by the 'originals'. Fortunately most of them discovered the benefits of the restful atmosphere and attuned themselves to the spirit of Infanta and, like the rest of us, just loved and cherished the place for its charm and uniqueness.

OPPOSITE TOP: Boating at the Breede River Mouth at Infanta. OPPOSITE BOTTOM: A room with a view – the accommodation on the Whale Trail is hard to beat and takes the 'rough' out of 'roughing it'. ABOVE: A southern right whale breaks the surface of a calm sea. You'll be able to see whales along the coast from June to November, but there are always early arrivals and late leavers! RIGHT: A seafood *potjie* with mussels, calamari and freshly caught fish is always the answer after an active day spent on the river.

The Breede River Lodge

The Breede River Lodge on the unspoilt bank of the mighty Breede River is a mariner's dream. Both the sea and the river beckon, and the fishing in the area is first rate. Who knows – if you have a good day, you might even make the Breede River Lodge Wall of Fame, a collage of photos of anglers (ranging from three years old upwards!) and their memorable catches. The lodge also charters boats, so if you tire of shore fishing you can head to the open seas on crafts with evocative names such as Goblin, Moby Dick, Play Boy *and* Sensation. *But there's more than just fishing – you can kayak, waterski and do some fantastic bird and whale watching. And, after a day in the fresh air and on the sea, there's nothing like a hearty meal. This is one of the Breede River Lodge's favourites.*

Chicken & shrimp curry

2 small onions (sliced)
1 small green pepper (sliced)
2 cloves garlic
2 medium tomatoes (diced)
4 cups water
2 tbsp chicken stock
2 tbsp Mrs Ball's hot chutney
1 tbsp cumin
1½ tbsp turmeric
2 tbsp curry powder
salt & pepper to taste
800 g chicken breast (cubed)
250 g shrimps
5 prawns

Sauté onions, pepper and garlic until soft. Add tomatoes and cook till pulpy. Add water, stock, chutney, dry ingredients and seasoning, and simmer. Brown chicken cubes in non-stick pan and add to sauce. Partly boil the shrimps and add just before serving. Garnish with one prawn each.

Sambals: tomato salsa

2–3 large diced tomatoes
1 small onion finely diced
1 clove garlic chopped fine
30 ml basil & origanum
30 ml olive oil
15 ml white wine vinegar
5 ml sugar
pinch of salt

Mix all of the above together. Serve with curry & rice, poppadums and fried banana.

TOP AND RIGHT: Early morning on the Breede River. ABOVE: Low tide at the Breede Mouth, with Infanta on the right and Witsand on the left. OPPOSITE: Aloes add a splash of colour to the vegetation on the river bank at Infanta (see p186). OVERLEAF: Spend any amount of time in the area and you'll soon get to see the many moods of the river. You'll also quickly find your favourite time of day, when the light is just right and the view from your *stoep* is everything you want it to be.

Witsand

Witsand, at the mouth of the Breede River, is a fisherman's paradise and many old – and not so old – sea salts have retired to the area to enjoy the whip of the wind and wide, open spaces. Residents have made small corners their own: look out for '*Oom Willie se bankie*' (with a plaque that identifies it as such) on the edge of a dune, or *Ouma's Tuin* built in and around an old boat.

The Whale Induna

To use a local expression, over the centuries the Breede 'has eaten' a number of the district's sons and daughters. The hazards are many and the forces where the ocean and river meet can be phenomenal. Local residents caution that there's a notoriously dangerous sandbar at the entrance to the river mouth that shifts position and has caught a number of people unawares. More recently, the sandbar resulted in the tragic death of Peter Esterhuizen, also known as the Whale Induna – a real Witsand local with enough *gees* to fill one of the Barry's old packing sheds that now stand so empty.

Peter's story, and his love for the whales that frequent the bay, is well documented in the beautifully made video *The Whale Induna*. His passion for these huge mammals was kindled in the early 1990s when he helped rescue a southern right whale trapped in the river. Days later when Peter was out on his boat he saw the same whale he had saved, but this time she had her calf with her and Peter believed she had come to show him her offspring – and thank him for rescuing her.

From then on, Peter believed he had discovered an unusual type of communication with the whales and those who experienced a boat-based whale watching trip with him will never forget this special connection between mammal and man. The video captures how, time and again, all Peter had to do was go out to sea, switch to neutral and wait for the whales to appear all around him. He believed they recognised his voice or the sound of his boat's engine.

But, read any of the old books on the Overberg, and you'll know that life is hard and elemental and Peter's idyll wasn't to last. Just six months after marrying his partner, Lesley, Peter died trying to tow another boat to safety. Of course, it was the perfect ending for a man who couldn't get up in the morning without looking at the sea to see if the whales were there.

The bay Peter loved so dearly has been declared a whale sanctuary and nursery, and boats are banned from the area where the whales breed, a whale watching outpost has been built on the shore in his memory. For Lesley and their son Senna, Peter's memory lives on forever.

Favourites

You can't leave the area without ...

- Catching a ride on the only hand-drawn pont left in South Africa and as the water glides quietly by sparing a thought to Moxie Dunn who pulled the pont by himself for close to three decades (see p179).
- Getting up at first light to do some serious bird-watching in the Breede Estuary.
- Going down the river on an organised trip with a reputable company. You can tackle the rapids, work your biceps doing some paddling, fall out a couple of times and then sit around a fire at night discussing the thrill of the day's adventures.
- Visiting the pretty Barry Church at Port Beaufort. Take a walk around the small graveyard and make a note of the dates of the births and deaths. By all accounts, you were old if you made it past 40 years of age.
- Having a Woodstock flashback and going to the Savannah Up the Creek Music Festival to catch some of the best South African bands in action.
- Watching the whales from the rocks at Infanta (see p187).
- Tagging and releasing a whopping cob. Don't forget to take a quick photo before you toss the fish back!
- Doing the spectacular Whale Trail in the De Hoop Nature Reserve. Along with the Otter Trail, this is becoming a hike every passionate walker needs to notch off on his or her walking stick (see p186).

ABOVE: A boat makes its way through early morning mist on the river. RIGHT: The Breede River is tidal for up to 60 kilometres from the mouth. CENTRE MIDDLE: The river valley is fertile and for centuries farmers from the area used to export their goods by boat back to the growing city of Cape Town. Today, some local farmers have turned their attention to pig and ostrich farming (see p187). CENTRE BOTTOM: The river banks at Infanta. OPPOSITE TOP LEFT: Twitchers have plenty to look forward to – birdlife is abundant and the Lower Breede River Conservancy is doing everything possible to protect this heritage (see p183). OPPOSITE TOP RIGHT: Detail from a private home at Infanta. MIDDLE: Sheep farming has always played an integral role in the history of the Overberg (see p124). BOTTOM: The pont at Malgas (see p179).

Contact numbers

Malgas and Witsand Tourism: 028-514-2770

Breede River Dream Cruises: 028-542-1049
De Hoop Nature Reserve: 028-542-1253
Felix Unite (Up the Creek Music Festival and Breede River rafting trips): 021-670-1300
Lower Breede River Conservancy: 021-712-0868
Potberg Nature Reserve: 028-542-1114

Where to stay

www.overberginfo.com
Barry's Holiday Accommodation (Witsand): 028-537-1717
Breede River Lodge (Witsand): 028-5371631
Malgas Hotel and Conference Centre: 028-542-1049
Mudlark Guest House (Breede River): 028-542-1161
Tides River Lodge (near Malgas): 028-542-1018
Waterkloof Guesthouse (Breede River): 028-722-1811

Overberg Annual Events and Climate

Town	Events	When to visit
Betty's Bay (See p39)	• Carols by Candlelight – Harold Porter National Botanical Garden (Dec) • Summer sunset concerts Harold Porter Botanical Garden (Dec)	Enjoy birding, walking, hiking and swimming in summer; horse riding, rock climbing and canoeing in autumn. From June to November whales and dolphins are regularly seen between Rooiels and Kleinmond. **Summer average: 26°C Winter average: 16°C**
Bredasdorp (See p124)	• Agricultural Show (Feb) • Foot of Africa Marathon (Oct)	Visit throughout the year! The area has excellent beaches that are great for fishing. Bird watching opportunities are always good. Spot the whales between June and November, while the fynbos is in bloom throughout the year. (This applies to full Cape Agulhas region: Elim (see below and p125) Napier (see below and p120), Struisbaai (see below and p104), L'Agulhas (p106) and Arniston (p94)) **Summer average: 20°C Winter average: 14°C**
Caledon (See p114)	• Wild Flower Show (Sept) • Christmas Light Festival (Dec)	Every season has its own charm. Autumn offers clear, warm days ideal for exploring the region. It's cold in winter, but also very green and the perfect time for soaking in the hot water springs. In spring the landscape is transformed by yellow canola fields, and summer offers excellent outdoor activities. **Summer average: 26°C Winter average: 12°C**
Elgin (See p16)	• Open Gardens (Nov)	This is a year-round holiday destination. Visit an apple packing shed, try local wines and remember to buy a bunch of flowers at one of the hothouses on your way home. **Summer average: 20°C Winter average: 13°C**
Elim (See p125)	• Heritage Festival (Aug)	See Bredasdorp above
Gansbaai (See p76)	• Crayfish Derby (Apr) • Lighthouse to Lighthouse Endurance Cycle ride (Apr) • Fees van die Ganse (Jul) • Christmas Craft Markets (Dec) • Dangerpoint Half Marathon (Dec)	June to November is whale season and there are both land- and boat-based whale watching opportunities. Shark viewing is good all year round. The best weather is in February and March when there is little or no wind. **Summer average: 20°C Winter average: 11°C**
Genadendal (See p147)	• Easter Sunday Sunrise Service (Mar) • Children's Festival (Aug) • Heritage Day Celebrations and Museum open day (Sept) • Christmas Eve Candlelight Service (Dec)	Visit all year round for the scenic beauty, but especially in autumn when the oak trees turn to gold. Nearby Greyton is an ideal country getaway in winter, offering many outdoor activities as well as fireside relaxation in quaint B&Bs and lodges (see p138). Visit in October for the annual rose festival. **Summer average: 26°C Winter average: 14°C**
Hermanus (See p52)	• Greater Hermanus Showcase (Apr) • Food and Wine Fair (Aug) • Kalfiefees (Afrikaans Arts, Culture and Language) • The Fernkloof Wildflower Show (Sept) • Whale Festival (Sept)	From July to November the whales are frolicking as close as 20 metres from shore. In September and October there's the added bonus of seeing calving and mating behaviour. November has wonderful summer days and February and March offer blissful weather ideal for the beach. **Summer average: 26°C Winter: 14°C**
Kleinmond (See p37)	• Total Sports Challenge (Jan) • Gravity River Festival (Aug) • Tourism Golf Day (Oct) • Nelson Mandela President's Golf Cup (Nov) • Christmas Market (Dec)	See Betty's Bay above
Napier (See p120)	• Patat Festival (June) • Horse and Cart Festival (Nov)	See Bredasdorp above
Pringle Bay (See p39)	• Kogelberg Mountain Race (Sept) • Hangklip Half Marathon (Dec)	See Bredasdorp above
Stanford (See p80)	• Western Province Canoe Union Annual Hermanus to Stanford Race (Apr/May) • Birding Fair (Oct) • Welsh Pony Show (Nov)	Every season has something to offer. The village is close to lovely beaches, while the river is fantastic to laze beside and for bird watching. There are excellent restaurants, a brewery and a dairy. The fynbos is exceptional and there are plenty of hikes and 4x4 routes for the adventurous. **Summer average: 25°C Winter average: 12°C**
Struisbaai (See p104)	• Yellowtail Festival (Mar)	See Bredasdorp above
Swellendam (See p158)	• Swellendam Show (Mar) • Swellengrebel Fly-Inn (Mar) • Swellendam Half Marathon (May) • K2 Canoe Marathon (Sept) • Bowls Classic (Sept) • Up the Creek Music Festival (Feb)	Visit in summer when the gardens are lush and the shady oaks line the streets. No matter how hot it is outside you can always escape into the cool old buildings. Winter is good for enjoying the cosy restaurants and big log fires. **Summer average: 28°C Winter average: 18°C**
Zuurbraak (See p166)	• Church Birthday Festival (Mar) • Tourism Festival (Sept)	All year round. December to February is the best time for hiking along the Buffeljags River while you listen to the birds and enjoy breathtaking views of the Langeberg Mountains. During autumn you can enjoy a donkey cart ride between the oaks. **Summer average: 25°C Winter average: 10°C**

Glossary

alikreukel: periwinkle
bakkies: open trucks/vans
bankie: little bench, seat
bankrotskap: bankruptcy
braai: barbeque
boep: paunch
boer: farmer
bokkoms: dried fish, usually harders
bord: plate
braai: barbecue
dorpies: small towns
droster: deserter
fees: festival
frikkadelle: meat balls
gebore: born
gees: spirit
gewone: ordinary
groot: big
hare: hair
hengelaars: anglers
hoek: corner
kaalvoet: barefoot
karretjies: carts
klein: small
kos: food
kraal: corral, pen
kreef: crayfish
kuier: visit
leiwater: irrigation water
lekker: good, nice
manne: men
mense: people
moerse: huge
Nagmaal: Holy Communion
omie: Uncle
opstal: homestead, farm premises
orkes: band/orchestra
ouens: blokes, chaps
ouma: grandma
oupa: grandpa
pap: porridge
pas op: watch out
perlemoen: abalone
platteland: countryside
skaars: scarce
skelms: rogues, crooks
slote: ditches, gutters
soetpatats: sweet potatoes
sommer: for no particular reason, just
strand: beach
tannie: aunt
tee en koek: tee and cake
toetsbaan: test range
tuin: garden
tuisnywerheid: home industry
veld: field, countryside
velskoen: rawhide shoe
vis: fish
vlaktes: plains
vlei: small lake/marsh/estuary
vleis: meat
volop: plentiful
ware: true, real
weeskind: orphan

Other terms:
Fynbos: 'fine bush' – indigenous vegetation occurring in the southwestern Cape.
Khoekhoen: The acceptable term referring to the indigenous pastoralists formerly called Khoikhoi (known as Hottentots in the early days of the colony).
Khoisan: Collective term used to describe the Khoekhoen and San peoples.
Overstrand: Term used by Overbergers to refer to the region's coastal areas.

References

1. *Apples Of The Sun*, by Phillida Brooke Simons. Published by Fernwood Press, 1999.

2. *Biography of Sir Antonie Viljoen*, by Mignonne Breier. Published by the Rawbone-Viljoen family, 1991.

3. *Breede River Revelations*, by Chris Mellish. Published by IBD Publishers, 1996.

4. *Cape Cottages*, by James Walton. Published by Intaka, 1995.

5. *Cape Peninsula South African Wild Flower Guide 3*, by Mary Maytham Kidd. Published by the Botanical Society of South Africa, 1996.

6. *Forgotten Corners of the Cape*, by Molly D'Arcy Thompson. Published by Timmins, 1981.

7. *Hermanus – A guide to the 'Riviera of the South'*, by Jose Burman. Published by Human & Rousseau, 1989.

8. *Hermanus Stories I – 1724–2001*, by SJ du Toit. Published by SJ du Toit, 2001.

9. *Illustrated Guide to the Southern African Coast*. Published by AA The Motorist Publications, 1988.

10. *Overberg*, by Anna Rothmann and John Warner. Published by Haum, 1983.

11. *The Overberg Explorer – A guide for Environment-orientated Travel in the Cape Overberg*, by Ann and Mike Scott. Published by Overberg Conservation Services, 2001.

12. *Overberg Outspan – A Chronicle of People and Places in the South Western Districts of the Cape*, by Edmund H. Burrows. Published by the author in co-operation with the Swellendam Trust, 1988.

13. *Somewhere Over the Rainbow – Travels in South Africa*, by Gavin Bell. Published by Abacus, 2000.

14. *Stanford Stories*, by SJ du Toit. Published by Milkwood Communications, 2000

15. *Tree of Life – The story of Cape Fruit*, by Siegfried Stander. Published by Saayman & Weber, 1983.

PREVIOUS SPREAD RIGHT: The De Hoop Nature Reserve (see p186) is an important conservation site for the Cape mountain zebra. RIGHT AND FAR RIGHT: De Mond Nature Reserve is home to some of South Africa's most endangered coastal birds, such as the African black oystercatcher (see p42). MONTAGE OVERLEAF: In the early to mid-1900s, before the introduction of fishing quotas, there was no shortage of fish in the waters of the Overstrand. Black-and-white photographs from the Hermanus Old Harbour Museum, and sepia holiday snaps taken by the Zoutendyk family at Witklip, clearly illustrate this abundance.

Index

Note: Page numbers in italics refer to photographs.

PREVIOUS SPREAD: The Elgin and Grabouw Country Club has one of the most magnificent settings in South Africa for playing – or watching – a game of cricket.
RIGHT: Groups of African sacred ibises – such as these at the Bot River Lagoon – are often seen flying in a characteristic 'V' formation over estuaries and vleis.
OPPOSITE: Walker Bay is famous for its beautiful beaches, which are instantly recognisable.